Leveraging DIVERSITY at Work

How to Hire, Retain and Inspire
a Diverse Workforce for
Peak Performance and Profit

KIM OLVER & SYLVESTER BAUGH

Chicago, Illinois

Leveraging Diversity at Work: How to Hire, Retain and Inspire a Diverse Workforce for Peak Performance and Profit ©2006 by Kim Olver & Sylvester Baugh

Published by:
Inside Out Press
PO Box 2666
Country Club Hills, IL 60478
insideoutpress.com

Ordering info:
708-957-6047
info@coachingforexcellence.biz

Cover design: Dunn + Associates Design
Interior design & typesetting: Folio Bookworks

Printed in the U.S.A.

Publisher's Cataloging-in-Publication Data

Olver, Kim.

Leveraging diversity at work : how to hire, retain and inspire a diverse workforce for peak performance and profit / Kim Olver & Sylvester Baugh. -- Chicago, Ill. : Inside Out Press, 2006.

p. ; cm.

ISBN-13: 978-0-9774388-4-6
ISBN-10: 0-9774388-4-8
Includes bibliographical references and index.

1. Diversity in the workplace. 2. Employees--Recruiting.
3. Employee retention. 4. Personnel management.
5. Multiculturalism. I. Baugh, Sylvester. II. Title.

HF5549.5.M5 O58 2006
658.3008--dc22   0607

Contents

Acknowledgements

We'd like to start by thanking Marcella Finnerty, without her there would likely be no *Leveraging Diversity at Work*. Marcella attended one of our diversity workshops and asked Kim afterwards if she could recommend some reference materials that approached diversity as we did during our workshop. Kim didn't have any answers for her. She didn't know of any so that night, Kim decided she would write this book. And that was it's conception.

We also need to thank each other for sharing our lives, perceptions and experiences. Without that open sharing, we wouldn't grow and evolve. We are eternally grateful for the learning opportunities.

Next, we need to thank our Reality Therapy and Choice Theory® instructors and friends. Our ideas on diversity have been shaped by our training in Choice Theory®, which has been taught to us by its founder, Dr. William Glasser. Those Reality Therapists who have influenced our growth and development are: Dr. William Glasser, Nancy Buck, Al Katz, Linda Harshmann, Cathy Curtiss, Steven English, Tom Smith, Marty Price, Pat Robey, Dick Hawes, Bob Sullo, Ellen Gélinas, Bob Hoglund, Bob Wubbolding, Denise Hunter, Fitz-George Peters and Jon Erwin.

Over the years, we had wonderful supervisors who saw our vision and supported the work we did in the area of diversity—Linda Solano, Gary Leofanti, Teresa Storer and Bernadette Maune.

We thank anyone who has even been in our diversity workshops because we always learn something new whenever we come together with a new group of people. Our own lives are enhanced and we gain new material for future writing and educating.

We want to acknowledge Dr. R.E.S.P.E.C.T., also known as Marcus C. Gentry, for the chapter he added to this book, as well as the contribution he makes to the struggle for equality everywhere and the specific education he provides young men of color.

We want to thank our friends and family who provided us with material for our book—Patty Hunt, Dave Olver, Kyle Olver, Lawanda Baugh, Kayla Baugh, Takiya Caradine, Chester Jackson, Debbie Street and many others.

We want to thank the pioneers in the field of diversity who came before us. It is on their great shoulders that we stand.

There were also those who helped us bring the book to life by reading chapters and offering their help and suggestions—Nancy Hankins, Denise Daub, Jane Elliott, Cecilia Chavez, Sondra Thiederman, and Leslie Wright.

And last but not least is our team of professionals who went above and beyond in service delivery—John Eggan, publishing educator; Liz Tufte, interior designer; Graham Van Dixhorn, copywriter; Kathi and Hobie Dunn, cover designers; and Despina Gurlides, our phenomenal editor. Without these professionals and their dedication to their craft, our book would be sitting in boxes in our garages instead of flying off the shelves.

We are so excited to be learners in this diversity journey with you. We sincerely hope our message will penetrate all that is happening around you in such a way that you will embark on your own journey. Do one small thing each day that will help bring people closer together instead of pulling them apart. Perhaps our paths will one day cross.

Introduction

Would you like to expand your business? Would you like your business to grow in character, as well as profit? Are you ready to invest in your business? This book was written to give you the tools to do just that. *Leveraging Diversity at Work* is a concept that will propel you and your company to the next level.

Companies often recognize the need for diversity training after a major incident. Sometimes this incident is as harmless as a team not functioning well together due to differences amongst its members. Other times this incident may be as serious as a discrimination lawsuit with expensive litigation costs. Diversity training can act as a preventive measure, decreasing the likelihood of such incidents happening.

While many companies recognize the value of diversity training, they tend to stop too soon. A diversity initiative is going to require much more than an annual training. It will require preparing your employees' minds and hearts to embrace difference. This does not occur in a single day's training.

Our book is designed to start at a very basic level. The early chapters are written to help even the most conservative members of your workforce understand what it may be like for a member of a minority culture. We work at helping people develop the empathy necessary to understand that minorities are suffering as a result of inequity and injustice.

Until your employees begin to develop some empathy for the other side— majority culture for minorities, as well as minorities for the majority culture—it is unlikely that any amount of training will help the situation. When people enter a new situation with their hearts and minds already closed, it is almost impossible to get them to consider another way. Our hope is that this book will open people to a new way of relating to members of other cultures.

Dr. Adela A. Allen once said, *"We should acknowledge differences, we should greet differences, until difference makes no difference anymore."* [1] Dr. Allen is acknowledging the importance of difference but is advocating that we appreciate and honor differences until certain differences will no longer be associated with great power. In this book, we provide information that shows the importance of utilizing diversity to grow your business. We explain the importance of the majority, as well as the minority culture making changes to bring about an effective diversity mix. We share many of our personal experiences because we believe that they will enlighten and encourage you to move in the direction of embracing diversity.

We (Kim and Sylvester) continue to learn from each other everyday, as well as from the people we have in our diversity trainings, and those we meet in our everyday lives. We share our stories because they were pivotal learning experiences for us, and we hope you may vicariously share in that learning process. We want you to know that putting yourself "out there" on a cultural competence journey can at times be terrifying, but it is also hugely rewarding. We don't always do things perfectly. We have made and continue to make many mistakes as we go. There is no perfection on this path. We hope that you, like us, will embrace the concept of learning from your mistakes, because there will be more than a few.

We believe that the solution to the diversity divide lies with majority and minorities alike. However, although all parties involved must play a significant role in rectifying the problem, the majority culture needs to take the initiative in moving toward diversity.

In this book, you will find confirmation for the many things that you are already doing right. Celebrate these things! However we hope that you will not only look for areas of strength that your company has, but that you will also critically examine those areas of your business where you can make improvements. Taking an analytical, objective look at your company's policies, practices, and informal networks may be difficult, but it is absolutely necessary if you are serious about moving your company to a position where its diversity can be leveraged.

This book will encourage you to look inside to find the places that are blocking you and your staff from effectively embracing diversity. Once you are able to identify these obstacles, this book will provide the steps that you and your employees can take to obtain and maintain an effective, harmonious, diverse workforce.

Many companies have chosen to avoid the idea of embracing diversity for two main reasons: They do not recognize the need for it and the effort is too great. In this book, we make a case as to why it is imperative to create and maintain a diverse workforce, and we simplify the process for you.

Leveraging Diversity at Work is about looking at yourself and your business in a more impartial way. The main asset of your business is your workforce. The more diverse the workforce, the more diverse your customer base. As you turn these pages, you will begin a journey toward understanding the power of diversity. Enjoy your journey. Our hope is that after reading this book you will be ready to see how difference can make a difference in your bottom line!

Respectfully,

Kim Olver

Sylvester Baugh

What Is Culture?

When someone asks you to share an important aspect of your culture, what comes to mind? Kim remembers the first time someone asked her that question. As a member of the white, majority culture in the United States, her first thought was that she doesn't have a "culture"; it is all simply a part of her life.

Upon closer scrutiny, the first place she looked for her culture was in her ethnic background: German, Scotch, Welsh, and English. However, she couldn't think of anything that was a part of her childhood that came from her ethnic heritage. The truth was she didn't know much about her heritage. She didn't know what aspects might be attributable to different ethnic backgrounds. All Kim knew was what occurred in her immediate family.

Culture is not Always Conscious

We are often unaware of our culture because it is so much a part of who we are; we simply think of our culture as "normal." It is something we take for granted—similar to the air we breathe. Culture simply *is*. The only time we really become acutely aware of our culture is when we leave it and enter another's, or when we come into contact with someone who does things differently than we do. Then, and only then, do we really begin to think about culture. Often our total unquestioning acceptance of our culture may tell us that people who do things differently are "wrong" and not simply "different." By strongly accepting our own culture, we may alienate others with different cultural backgrounds.

Culture is Everything

After having been exposed to people from different cultures, Kim now understands that every human being has a culture—even she does. She now possesses the ability to examine her own culture and the things that make her uniquely Kim. Culture is a total way of life. It's everything that is familiar to us: our religion, beliefs, values, food, clothing, hairstyle, celebrations, family relationships, discipline practices, dating patterns, holidays, gender roles, and hobbies. Everything that comprises what we know, what we are exposed to, how we do things, and what *feels* right to us, is part of our culture. The person we are—and the person we are becoming—is greatly influenced by our cultural information and experiences.

People typically think of race and ethnicity when first asked about their culture. Because of the long and chronicled history of race relations in this country, it is almost impossible to avoid this discussion. We are not suggesting that racial issues do not exist in the United States. However, we'd like people to expand this definition to include the sum total of all one's life experiences, including spiritual beliefs, political affiliation, parenting style, geography, education level, socio-economic status, gender roles, media valued and viewed, customs, traditions, holidays, family interactions, travel and exposure to other cultures, criminal activity in the neighborhood, sexual practices, and community involvement. The list is endless; to learn everything about someone else's culture is a monumental, if not impossible, task.

Culture Starts at Birth

Culture begins at the moment of birth. Most of us, in the United States, were born in a hospital. However, being born in a hospital is not the only option. Personal choice or circumstance may dictate a hospital, a midwife at home, an unassisted birth at home, or a birth in an alley or public restroom somewhere. Our first experiences immediately after birth begin to shape who we become. It may even be argued that our culture begins in the uterus, based upon the environment in the womb.

For the purpose of this discussion, let's say culture begins at the moment of birth. Imagine a Caucasian woman who gives birth to a Caucasian baby girl and then gives her up for adoption to an African-American couple. Will that child grow up in a Caucasian or an African-American culture? That child will be raised in an African-American culture. Culture is learned; it is not biological or innate.

The process by which we acquire our culture is known as acculturation. This is not a conscious process used to shape the child, but a subconscious one based on prior knowledge and experience of what is best for the upbringing of that child.

Our Judgments of Others Originate in our Culture

This is why we often find ourselves judging how others discipline their children in public. You are sitting in a restaurant with your family enjoying a nice family meal, and directly across from your table is another family also enjoying a family meal. The children of the other family are speaking loudly, throwing food, and not using "proper" table manners. You become annoyed with this family and ask to be moved. Now that you have moved, you begin to judge their behavior. You wonder how people could allow their children to act in such a way in public. Is it also possible that they are wondering why your family is so quiet and reserved? Because of acculturation, each family has a different way of behaving.

In *Beyond Culture*, Edward T. Hall states, "Culture is man's medium; there is not one aspect of human life that is not touched and altered by culture."[1] Culture determines the way we think, feel, act, perceive the world, respond to situations, and problem solve. Culture consists of values, beliefs, and rules of conduct. Culture reflects traditions that have been passed from one generation to another. Culture is dynamic and changes over time.

In 2001, Kim traveled with a group of colleagues to Australia. When they exited the airport in Sydney, one of her colleagues said, "Look, they drive on the wrong side of the road here!" Wrong is a very strong word with lots of judgment and self-righteousness attached. Kim wondered what might have happened if her friend had attempted to drive on her "right" side of the road in Australia! What seems strange or wrong in one cultural context is exactly the correct thing to do in another. Imagine instead the simple statement, "Look, they drive on the left side of the road here!"

What seems logical, sensible, important, and reasonable in one culture may seem irrational, ridiculous, unimportant, and unreasonable to an outsider. For example, Kim remembers a time when Sylvester was visiting her home in rural Pennsylvania. Sylvester, Kim, and her two children had left the house for the day to go on an outing. When they returned, Kim discovered that her kitchen door had been left open. She asked the boys, "Which one of you was the last one out of the house and didn't close the door?" And then she proceeded to walk into the house.

Sylvester became very agitated and told her not to go into the house but to call the police instead. Kim had no idea why he was so worried and thought he was seriously overreacting! After all, it was obvious to her what had happened. Someone had simply failed to close the door. However, in Sylvester's world, it was more likely that someone had invaded her house and may still have been inside. Sylvester and Kim come from two different cultures—urban and rural. Although they found each other's concern, or lack thereof, unusual, in their respective cultures their unique positions made perfect sense.

At some point in our life we take all the knowledge we've acquired and all the experiences we've had and develop a code of values that feels totally right for us. This is a normal, healthy process of development. However, the next step we generally take although normal, is definitely not healthy or helpful toward building relationships with people who are different from us. After we decide what values are right for us, we take a gigantic step forward and develop ideas and strong opinions about what is right for other people as well. This is where the danger occurs. Can we ever really know what is right for another person? How can we, if we haven't had exactly the same experiences? Values are very subjective: There is no right or wrong; there is simply what's right or wrong for the person who holds them.

Co-Culture Value Clashes

Within all cultures lie smaller groups of people who band together because of similar values, beliefs, and practices. We used to call these sub-cultures but now the politically correct term is either co-culture or mini-culture, to avoid the prefix "sub" which implies beneath or less than.

People can belong to many different co-cultures within their over-arching culture. For example, Kim identifies herself as an American—her main, overarching culture. She is also a Caucasian, a Methodist, a parent, an entrepreneur, a musician, a counselor, an author, a liberal democrat, and a heterosexual female, among other things. Depending on circumstances, she will draw from these co-cultures differently.

When the United States was attacked on September 11, 2001, Kim experienced a value conflict based on her association with different co-cultures. Initially, as a member of the American culture she, like many others, purchased a flag to put up in her yard and a decal for the window of her car, to illustrate the unity this country was feeling through patriotism. As an American Kim was shocked, outraged, and sought retribution. Like the majority of Americans, she wanted revenge. Find Bin Ladin and end terrorism!

However, soon after, her counseling ethics and Christian values chimed in to add different voices to the melee. What would God want us to do? Jesus said, "Turn the other cheek"[2] and did not endorse the Old Testament's, "an eye for an eye" philosophy.[3] Then, as a counselor, Kim began to wonder how people could hate Americans so much to perpetrate such an extreme act of violence. It was not that difficult to get a preliminary answer when she began thinking how the "have-nots" in this world have tended to dislike and even hate those who have. However, she believes that there is much we still don't understand due to the incredible lack of accurate and conclusive information that exists.

Kim does know that if her child were being bullied by someone much bigger and stronger than he is, she would advise him to defend himself in any way possible. When fighting someone with an unfair advantage, the rules of fair combat make no sense. Is there a parallel? Kim doesn't know, but she does believe in Stephen Covey's 5th Habit of Highly Effective People: "Seek first to understand; then to be understood."[4]

Understanding another's culture can be complex; it requires a great deal of time and effort. As we will discuss later in the book, we attempt to understand and categorize others by creating, in our minds, who we think they are and what they stand for. Without taking the time to get to know them, we formulate an opinion and then believe we know and understand them.

We use the 9-11 example not to provide an analysis of the World Trade Center attack, but to offer the understanding that values may conflict with each other, depending on one's culture and membership in various co-cultures. When this occurs, much thought and deliberation are required to sort it all out. We may even resign from a particular co-culture, if the conflict becomes too great.

In the world of business, one of the biggest cultural conflicts concerns time. Sylvester remembers he would get very angry when clients didn't show up on time for their appointment. He would pace the floor and peer through his blinds right up until the point they arrived. This behavior was based on the fact that his cultural belief is that 10:00 o'clock means exactly 10:00—not five minutes later. In his culture, tardiness is sometimes considered a sign of disrespect. If he transfers his perception of tardiness to others, then this affects how he views them. This can and does create conflict for many co-workers, managers, and administrators.

Although culture is a big part of our existence, it is not given the degree of attention it deserves in the workplace. Cultural differences are at the heart of the problems within most companies. Since many of the people who work together have different cultural backgrounds, there are going to be some challenges.

Sylvester once worked for a company that provided social services to low-income residents. Since there were few employees, everyone worked long hours to keep the company running. The problem was that some people believed they worked harder than others. However, those who were accused of not working as hard believed that they were working just as hard as everyone else—their acculturation of work was just different. Each side was trying to prove that their cultural position was the correct one.

Think about a time when you had a disagreement with someone you loved. The argument may have gotten very heated and you may have become emotional. Because you cared about this person, a part of you really wanted to reconcile. You remembered how it felt when you and this person were in sync and communicating well. You laughed together, you joked together, and sometimes you even cried together. Why can't you find your way back there? You argue, you raise your voice, you may even use profanity, but in your heart you want the peace and calm of the relationship you remember— but there is something that is prohibiting you from getting there. Even though you can remember the good feelings, you can't seem to overcome your acculturation which tells you to convince others to see things the way you do—the "right" way.

Culture can Inhibit Objectivity

We typically don't examine other cultures from an objective point of view; we examine them based on what we know and what feels comfortable. It is our early childhood cultural lessons that set the tone for everything that we do and how we do it. Imagine being in an office where you are the only person who speaks English. Aside from the fact you would have difficulty communicating, you might tend to feel out of place—not because you don't speak their language but because they don't speak yours. You would believe your language is the best one and you wouldn't want to have to change or give up your language. You might allow your thoughts to lean towards having everyone else change, as opposed to you changing. Although there are times when the majority will influence a person to assimilate, acculturation will encourage that person to remain rooted in his or her culture and to be certain he or she is right.

Our ability to connect and stay connected in an effective way which satisfies our needs is dependent upon our ability to become more objective. Our culture has shaped us, but we must understand that it is only right for us and not everyone else. When we can become more accepting of different cultures, we will have a better chance of establishing more harmonious relationships. By taking a more objective look at our culture, we give ourselves the opportunity to grow, and we allow others the opportunity to be who they are.

The next chapter will present different cultural factors and characteristics, and will discuss how these characteristics strongly influence our thoughts and behaviors in interpersonal exchanges with other people.

Cultural Factors

There are many factors to consider when examining culture. We would like to discuss two main types of factors, which have different and complex effects on people:

- the primary and secondary dimensions of diversity

- the visible and invisible characteristics of culture

Primary and Secondary Dimensions of Diversity

Primary dimensions of diversity are unalterable and have an extremely powerful effect on a person. These are the characteristics that a person has no choice about and cannot be changed, such as: race, gender, age, ethnicity, sexual orientation, and certain physical abilities and qualities.

While there are extreme examples where these factors have been changed, these exceptions are quite rare. Transgendered people have been known to change their gender, for example. Others alter the appearance of their age through cosmetic procedures, but no medical procedure has yet been able to actually change a person's age. It has also been argued that sexual orientation can be changed. However, while people may be able to change their sexual behavior, their attraction to a specific gender, or in the case of bisexuals to both genders, remains unchanged.

It is our belief that a person's sexual orientation is a biological/genetic attraction that cannot be altered by a sheer act of will. How would it feel if society suddenly decided that homosexuality was the "right" way to be, and everyone who was heterosexual had to engage in homosexual relationships or else experience severe consequences? Ridiculous! While people might be able to engage in homosexual activity if enough societal pressure is applied, the fact doesn't change that their preference is for members of the opposite sex.

The secondary dimensions of diversity are also significant in shaping a person's life, but these can be altered. Some examples are sexual behavior, choice of profession, socioeconomic status, military experience, marital status, location of home, religious beliefs, educational background, parental status, and political affiliation. As children we usually can't make these decisions for ourselves, and are influenced by the decisions that adults make for us. But as adults we have the privilege of making some decisions and choices in these areas.

Janet Elsea's research as documented in her book, *4 Minute Sell*, is very interesting.[1] Her research discovered the nine most important characteristics noticed by a person when first meeting someone new. In order of importance, they are: skin color, gender, age, appearance, facial expressions, eye contact, movement, personal space, and touch.

When we first encounter a person, we make decisions about how we will interact with him or her based on these nine characteristics. The first three items on the list fall into the category of primary dimensions of diversity. This means that we are primarily making assessments about people based upon conditions over which they have no control. We don't know about you, but Kim doesn't want to be judged solely on the fact that she is a white, 45 year-old female; similarly Sylvester prefers to be judged on characteristics other than his being a black, 44 year-old male.

The next six items on the list are culturally determined, which means that they are neither right nor wrong. These characteristics are simply what is comfortable and familiar in our world as we know and experience it. Should we be judging people based on these characteristics? We don't think so. We believe that we need to get to know people individually, so that our assessments of them have some depth and relevant content.

Visible and Invisible Characteristics

As we develop, we begin to recognize what is appealing to our eyes. We develop size preference. We develop hair length preference. We develop ethnic preference. Visible characteristics become very important to us. We begin to determine the kind of person with whom we would like to spend our lives, based on visible characteristics.

Many of these decisions are based on what we have been exposed to in the media. Magazines and television inundate us with information on looks. Commercials that promote beauty products and hair growth formulas can be seen all over the television. Even the ads promoting health spas typically promote how good your body will look if you become a member.

In her book, *First Impression Best Impression,* Dr. Janet G. Elsea reports that people focus on what they can see.[2] We are a visually driven society. You may have heard people say that looks don't matter; however, society and the media have put a premium on looking good. Most of our impressions of people are determined by what we see or hear from others and the media.

Information from the Social Issues Research Centre[3] confirms that the visual plays a major role in how we are viewed and treated:

- Attractive children are more popular, both with classmates and teachers. Teachers give higher evaluations to the work of attractive children and have higher expectations of them, which has serendipitously been shown to improve the attractive child's academic performance.

- Attractive applicants have a better chance of getting jobs, and of receiving higher salaries. (One U.S.

study found that taller men earned approximately $600 more per inch than shorter executives.)

- In court, attractive people are found guilty less often. When found guilty, they receive less severe sentences.

This bias for beauty operates in almost all social situations. We believe in the "what is beautiful is good" stereotype. We have an irrational but deep-seated belief that physically attractive people possess other desirable characteristics such as intelligence, competence, social skills, confidence, and even moral virtue. (The good fairy/ princess is always beautiful, while the wicked witch/stepmother is always ugly.) The visible is extremely important to us. This is why cosmetic procedures are so popular.

The American Society for Aesthetic Plastic Surgery (ASAPS), a national not-for-profit organization for education and research in cosmetic plastic surgery, annually conducts the nation's most authoritative survey of U.S. physicians performing cosmetic procedures. It reports that the number of cosmetic procedures in the United States increased by 44% in 2004, reaching nearly 11.9 million. Of these, the number of surgical procedures increased 17%, while the number of non-surgical procedures increased 51% from the previous year.[4] The most popular surgical procedure was liposuction; the most frequently performed non-surgical procedure was Botox injection.

"I believe at least some of this upward trend may be attributable to increased media coverage of plastic surgery in 2004," says ASAPS President Peter Fodor, MD, of Los Angeles. "People have had many more opportunities to see, first hand, what plastic surgery is like and what it can do for others. That can be a strong incentive for them to seek the same benefits by having cosmetic procedures themselves."

Although the visible characteristics are important to us, there are more powerful invisible human characteristics that we would like to discuss. When you get beyond a person's size, eye color, hair color, and overall beauty, there are other attributes that will play a part in the overall assessment of an individual. The difficulty with these characteristics is that they are well hidden, and may not be seen until a commitment has been made.

When people apply for jobs, they take time to enhance and accentuate their visible characteristics. They dress well, their hair and nails are done, and they present themselves in a way that might be appealing to their prospective employer, to increase their chances of employment. Many times this works, but the employer doesn't know about the invisible characteristics of the individual. What are their values? What are their morals? Our values and morals play a significant role in how we view others. Our invisible characteristics provide the motivation behind all of the visible behaviors in which we engage. They are what drive us.

On April 14th, 1912, a vessel hailed as "unsinkable," the Titanic, sank after colliding with an iceberg. Because ice is slightly less dense than water, only about one ninth of the total mass of an iceberg projects above the water; the rest of the iceberg lies concealed beneath the water. We can compare the visible and the invisible characteristics of a person to an iceberg. The tip of the iceberg represents the visible characteristics, while the portion of the iceberg underneath the water represents a person's invisible characteristics.

The invisible characteristics that we all possess are extremely strong, just as the part of the iceberg underneath the water is larger and stronger than the tip of the iceberg. These invisible characteristics carry more weight and are deceptive because people can't see them. Our invisible characteristics, determined by our values and morals, give us the confidence to act visibly. When we experience people and situations, these invisible characteristics will determine our behavior.

Sylvester remembers growing up in a household where there was an understood value: CHILDREN DO NOT GO INTO THE LIVING ROOM! The living room, with plastic on the furniture, was a place that was off limits to children. Guests were allowed to go into the living room, but he and his siblings were not. He grew to understand this as a way of life. This was a value that was hidden in his invisible.

One day while visiting a friend, Sylvester observed his friend's two younger siblings running into the living room. As he observed them jumping and playing in the living room, his invisible values sent him a message: What they were doing was not right, and if Sylvester didn't do something these kids were going to suffer major consequences. He immediately leapt from his seat and ran into the living room, ordering the children to come out and resume playing in a more "appropriate" part of the house. Soon after, his friend came in to question Sylvester as to what he was doing. Sylvester went on to explain, which caused his friend to laugh uncontrollably. Sylvester was informed that it was perfectly all right for the children to be in the living room. What had prompted Sylvester to be so visibly vocal? It was his invisible value of children not being permitted in the living room.

Although Sylvester felt completely justified in his assessment of the situation, he was wrong within that particular context. There are times when our invisible will give us a false sense of security, encouraging our visible to act within that comfort zone. We say things we shouldn't say and we do things we should not do, because our invisible tells us that not only is it acceptable, it's the "right" thing to do.

Many times in the workplace, co-workers are not able to control their invisible characteristics, often leading to verbal exchanges that may be damaging to a relationship. One of the fieriest coaches Sylvester has ever witnessed is former Indiana University and current Texas Tech basketball coach, Bobby Knight. Bobby is known for his temper, his antics, and his ability to achieve success as a coach. As a former athlete, Sylvester has often wondered what it would be like to play for someone like Bobby Knight. Obviously Coach Knight believes that public verbal confrontation is acceptable during a practice, game, or press conference. Since Sylvester believes that problems between two people should be handled in private, being coached by Mr. Knight might prove difficult for him. This is not to say that Mr. Knight's approach is right or wrong . . . it is just simply his approach. It is an approach with which he is comfortable and one that has brought him great coaching success. There most likely will be times when a different approach may be more advisable and effective, but unless people learn how to manage their invisible, they will always respond the way they feel most comfortable.

Managing one's invisible characteristics is extremely important. Although our invisible is at the root of our existence, we sometimes have to produce behaviors that are not products of those roots. It is important to understand the need to manage and control our thoughts and our actions.

When our invisibles get in the way, what others see in us is a judgmental nature. This never brings people closer together. Having positive and cooperative relationships in the workplace depend on a person's ability to manage his or her values in a way that doesn't come across as critical to another person.

How we view people often creates feelings about them, and these feelings encourage us to treat people a certain way. We all were acculturated with values of particular groups. There were statements made in our homes and communities that become fixed beliefs in our invisible. These beliefs influence how we treat people. If your belief system tells you that all women should be homemakers and caretakers, then you will consider a woman who wants a career to be wrong. It is so important for us to manage our beliefs and our behaviors. Remember, just because you feel a certain way, doesn't mean that you should act on it. Everyone is not punished for going into the living room.

In order for any company to be successful in launching a full-fledged diversity initiative, all employees must first develop a clear sense of cultural awareness. We have attempted to lay the foundation for this in the first two chapters. It is critical to be aware of how much culture permeates everything.

Another part of cultural awareness is the understanding that cultural differences do not represent one group doing something "wrong." Difference is simply that—different. No one group is right at the other's expense. This is an important understanding for management and workers to have in a workplace that is starting a diversity initiative.

We cannot get away from the invisible characteristics of diversity. They can actually make or break the camaraderie of a company. Employees come into an organization with their own values, morals, and beliefs. Although we don't sit down and formally assess them, they will reveal themselves in due time. During interviews, we do our best to assess the values of potential employees. We offer hypothetical scenarios and ask about their response to these situations. We ask about their past experiences and how they responded to them. We take these responses and we weigh them against not only what the company needs, but also what we agree to be the company culture. We then use this form of assessment to influence our decision-making.

After the hiring decision comes the introductory period. As in any new relationship, there is a period of time when people are getting to know each other. During this time, we become more aware of our own invisible characteristics. This is the time when we are attempting to make the best impression. We are more careful in managing our invisible because we don't want to do anything that will cause conflict or put the relationship in jeopardy. We work hard to prevent our invisible from influencing and manifesting itself in our visible—at least for a while until our comfort level increases. The more familiar we become in the relationship, the more we allow our invisible characteristics to become visible.

After a period of time, we believe the relationship can withstand disagreements or differences of opinion, and so we don't control our invisible as much as we did initially. The more we let down our guard, the more our invisible becomes apparent. We have taken the time to assess the relationship and to see if our true self will be accepted and if we can accept others. If our values and their values don't line up, we must find a way to manage how we feel so that it does not affect our ability to get the job done. The companies that achieve more—in terms of increased teamwork, productivity, and profit and decreased employee turnover—are the companies that stress the importance of truly understanding the position of others before expressing one's own position.

Our invisible is an important and powerfully influential aspect of who we are, but if we don't take the time to manage it, we can cause damage to the very relationships that are important to us. Although you may not value your boss's work ethic, it is important that you assess the strength of your relationship before you allow your invisible to be seen. Your inability to effectively manage your invisible could lead to your suspension or possible termination. It can also affect the overall mood of the company if your invisible and your boss' invisible are shown to be incompatible. This is why it is important to understand your morals, values, and beliefs, and to assess your relationships before you allow them to become visible.

In this chapter, we have discussed factors that are influential in our interactions with others. In the next chapter we will be discussing why visual information is so important and why it is we connect visually.

Why We Connect Visually

Of the five senses, many of us rely on vision the most to make sense of and to organize our perception of the world. In the case of visually impaired individuals, they will develop their other senses to a stronger degree.

Our Visual Sense is Primary

Phrases such as, "seeing is believing" and "what you see is what you get" indicate the importance of our visual sense. Our visual sense directly relates to our faith, belief, confidence, and assurance. We need to believe in the people who surround us, and the one way that we gage our level of belief is by what we see.

We spend time with our families—our spouses and children—on a regular basis. This time affords us the opportunity to get to know who they really are—their character and what they value. Although this is accomplished through a variety of means, what they show us and what we see is critical to our understanding of them.

We believe that when we look into a person's eyes we can see the truth revealed there. Whenever we are attempting to communicate with someone important to us, and we want them to understand the importance of our words, we will look him or her in the eyes and request the same kind of eye contact in return. When we tell our life partner for the first time that we love him or her, it is important to combine the seriousness and honesty of our emotions with a visual message.

Parents across the globe attempting to ascertain the truth from their children can be heard saying, "Look me in the eyes when you tell me that!" In many cultures, it is believed that we will be able to ascertain if the truth is being told by the strength and steadiness of our child's gaze.

Let's say that you have a 16 year-old son. You and your son have a great relationship. You spend a great deal of time together and you are proud of his accomplishments. Not only is he an A-student, but also a star athlete in football and baseball. On top of that, he volunteers at a local home for the elderly. One day while you are sitting at home, the telephone rings. A police officer informs you that your son has been arrested. The charge is armed robbery. When you hear this news, it is hard for you to believe it. How can this be true? This kind of behavior does not match the person whom you know your son to be. You refuse to believe this information because you didn't *see* him do it. We want to *see* the proof. We want to *view* the evidence. Our faith is not placed in the words of the police; it is placed solely on what we see, or in this case the absence of what we see. Being visually connected helps us understand and accept the truth.

Looking Good *is* Important

Being visually connected is also important because appearances—how someone or something looks—are important to us. Oftentimes we use visual cues to assess people whom we don't know.

Did you ever people-watch? What is it that makes people-watching so entertaining? People-watching is one of Kim's favorite pastimes. She loves to create stories about people's lives based on what she sees and observes. She knows absolutely nothing about them but she is able to concoct their entire fictional life story based on what they look like. People-watching can be very entertaining and hurts no one, as long as the people-watchers keep their comments and thoughts to themselves.

People-watching illustrates the importance of visible characteristics. Kim would have difficulty making up a story about a person whom she was unable to see. A visual picture is useful for us to begin making assumptions about another person.

Of course there is no way of knowing if our assumptions are correct. As much as we would like to believe that we have good insight into human behavior, it's most likely that the majority of our assumptions are incorrect. Why? Because the only thing we know is what the person looks like. What does someone's visible exterior tell us about the actual person? Nothing much, though we rely heavily on outer appearances in making our decisions about people.

Makeovers have become very prominent in this day and age. Some shows offer home makeovers while others promote physical makeovers. Television viewers are very interested in these makeover shows, as evidenced by their ratings, because makeovers enhance the visual appearance, and looking good is important.

Beauty is in the eye of the beholder. Although we understand the importance of values, morals, trust, and commitment, these attributes are often less important than a person's appearance.

Have you ever been single and interested in dating? When your friends ask you what you are looking for in a date, you most likely list certain admirable features, such as: a sense of humor, optimism, a sense of family, loyalty, honesty, trustworthiness, and kindness. But if a friend tells you that he or she knows the perfect person for you, what do you normally say? "Oh great! Maybe you can arrange for us to meet Friday night?" Probably not. It is more likely that you will ask, "What does he or she look like?" There is nothing more dreaded than the blind date whose best tag line is: "He/she is really nice."

Some people are really direct about their physical preferences. A woman may describe herself as desiring a man who is tall; a man may describe himself as a "leg man." Unfortunately, for many people these physical characteristics become the basis for choosing a mate.

So while personality characteristics are very important to the long term success of a relationship, most relationships never get beyond the initial hello unless there is some type of mutual physical attraction based on appearance.

Visual Connection

The Internet has really added a new dimension to the importance of being visually connected. We use the Internet for many things: purchasing cars, homes, and even finding that special someone. When signing up on web sites that offer dating services, most members include an extensive description of themselves, highlighting their physical attributes. They will also provide an overview of non-physical characteristics such as their personality, likes and dislikes, religious affiliations, and education status. Despite the fact that members provide these detailed descriptions about themselves, they are strongly encouraged to include a photograph. It is the photograph that will, in many cases, "seal the deal." The visual connection increases the likelihood that you are going to have success in finding that special someone. In fact, most people using Internet dating services won't even contact a person whose picture is not posted.

Years ago, telephone conferencing became a major tool of business. Businesses were able to communicate at the same time with several people from different parts of the world, completing many business deals without the added travel expenses. Although this technology was useful, it did not provide its participants with visual information. Video conferencing, on the other hand, allows participants to see the individuals with whom they are speaking. The fact that participants can see each other gives them an opportunity to read their faces and make conclusions about their emotional state. This was a step up from using the Internet, because videoconferencing allowed you to see actual, in the moment, movement and emotion. However, now the Internet is catching up with web conferencing which provides virtually the same service.

Visual connection is important not only in business but also in personal relationships. For example, if a relationship is not working and one person is considering ending the relationship, a face-to-face meeting is desired so that the emotion behind the words can be seen. This is also true when delivering an endearing message. We want someone who is expressing his or her innermost feelings about us to do it face-to-face.

Since visual connection is so important, it becomes imperative that we are viewed by others in a favorable way. Recently the National Basketball Association (NBA) instituted a dress code. This decision sparked a great debate amongst players and fans alike. Many fans did not believe that the NBA had the right to tell players how to dress. Some players called the decision racist, believing that the rules that were being instituted were directed against black players. There were many points of view on this issue. However, the NBA stated that it simply wanted to change the image of the players. It wanted the players' off-court attire to be more along the lines of a business person so that the world would view them more favorably.

Logos and Other Symbols

Many companies spend hundreds of thousands of dollars to create logos. A logo is the visual representation of the company. Many man hours and thousands of dollars go into making the decision about a logo because the visual connection is so important. Along with the logo come decisions concerning business cards, stationary, office furniture, interior decorating, and the decor of the corporate building.

The physical environment speaks volumes. When you are selecting paints, colors, and furniture for your business, it is important to take into account how these will be perceived by your customers. The ambiance that you create will go a long way toward building your company's reputation. Finally, businesses concern themselves with the appearance of their employees. Many companies have dress codes—some even requiring uniformity among the staff. The appearance of the physical environment and that of the employees are important factors in improving a company's visual connection.

Many designers today rely on their name or logo to encourage people to purchase their product. Designers, such as Tommy Hilfiger, have created logos that stand out; when the logo is displayed, the customer is automatically connected to the designer. The Nike "swoosh" has become synonymous with athletic attire. Their commercials always end with the logo because it's something many consumers have connected with.

Michael Jordan has his own line of athletic attire. For his clothing line to be successful, it had to be distinguished from Nike's. For many years Michael was Nike's chief spokesperson. Many would say that Michael was responsible for making the "swoosh" so easily recognized. Branching off to start his own line was challenging but Michael managed to pull it off. Michael's logo is a silhouette of him holding a basketball moving towards the basket for a dunk. Since this visual image is very familiar to Michael's fans, it has become a logo that works.

When an athlete's popularity begins to soar, companies will bid for the athlete's sponsorship of their product because they want their customers to have a visual connection to the rising star athlete. Athletes such as LeBron James and Michael Vick are today's hot commodities. Since society already accepts and approves of them, companies want them to market their products. It is therefore important for athletes to continue to look good. Many athletes hire individuals to make sure that their image stays clean so that they continue to be marketable. Kobe Bryant is an example of how an athlete's reputation can be damaged if society comes to view a person in a negative light.

One of the symbols that many people around the world connect with visually is the cross. Many of us will draw a spiritual conclusion about the individual wearing a cross. This visual symbol is supposed to say something about the individual who displays it, in much the same way as gang members display their colors. The point is that visual symbolism takes on a life of its own. This is not such a bad thing when it relates to inanimate objects. However, when making decisions about people based on their visual appearance, we need to evaluate the visual information and question its accuracy and validity.

Visual Input Aids Communication

Companies rely on the fact that their employees will engage in effective communication with each other and with management. Effective communication keeps the company operating and growing. However, it is important that most of the communication take place face-to-face. Personal, face-to-face communication is important because we connect visually with an individual's emotions. Our face and physical behavior will frequently tell a story that may not be heard in the words alone.

Research has shown that communication has both verbal and non-verbal components. The actual words we use comprise only 7% of the message we convey. The added vocal qualities we assign to these words in terms of tone, pitch, volume, and cadence comprise another 38% of the message. Guess what makes up the other 55% of the meaning of our expressed communication? You guessed it—our visual behavior: posture, eye contact, and facial expressions. Another interesting fact is that three-quarters of this visible behavior is based on what a person's face communicates during an exchange.[1]

Oftentimes, without even realizing, our facial expressions will convey our feelings. People who know us may pick up on nuances in our facial expressions that visually display how we are really feeling. There may be times when we raise our eyebrows in anger. Or we may be frightened and try not to show it, but our frozen facial expression gives us away.

There are times when employees or managers may have to deliver bad news. There was an incident when a company was faced with major cutbacks. After several meetings, management decided that they would lay off certain employees. The management team further decided to call these employees at home to inform them that they were being laid off. The reason for this decision was to avoid having disgruntled employees at work. This news was obviously devastating to the employees who were laid off. For most of them, the most significant concerns related to taking care of their families and being able to pay their bills. However, there was a young woman who was concerned about something totally different.

When she heard the news, she asked to come in and meet with the management team. The team agreed and the woman came into the office later that week. The management team quickly expressed their regrets for the decision, explaining what had occurred with the budget and what their plans were for the future. As she sat and listened, she began to cry. She shared that several years before she came to the company, she had gone through a divorce. After eight years of marriage her husband called her on the phone one day and told her he wanted a divorce. She stated that the feelings she had experienced then all came rushing back to her when she received the telephone call telling her that she was laid off. She had missed the opportunity to see her husband's face when he delivered his fateful news to her. She now wanted the opportunity to see the faces of her managers when they gave her the news. This way she would be able to tell if there was truly remorse in the decision. Although the words that were spoken delivered a disturbing outcome, she wanted the visual connection to better assess the situation.

It is important that managers understand the strength behind visible connections. We use emails and memos as ways to communicate with the largest number of people in the shortest amount of time. However, when individuals are given a visual experience, the words take on a more genuine meaning. Although you will not always have an opportunity to meet with people on a personal level, it is important to understand the power behind doing so.

Without the visual connection, the potential for miscommunication increases. A person can infer sarcasm into an email when it wasn't intended. A memo can communicate facts but not the emotion behind the decision. Whenever possible, it is worth the extra effort to communicate in person. It actually saves time in the long run that may be spent dealing with potential hurt feelings or clearing up any miscommunication. Although the Internet is a wonderful tool for communicating, without the visual connection much of the intended message can be lost.

In the next chapter, we will discuss how our values and beliefs (often based on visual information) quickly lead to righteousness, which never helps to connect people.

Values, Beliefs, and Righteousness

In Chapter 1, culture was defined as a total way of life. It follows that people's values and beliefs are shaped and influenced by their cultural experiences. Values and beliefs that dictate what is right and wrong form the foundation of a particular culture. Many of these values and beliefs are often not conscious. We must therefore examine our values and beliefs so that we can understand how they influence our interactions with others, especially with members of cultural groups that are different from us.

Examining one's own value system is much like proof reading one's own writing. A person may not always see what is actually there, but rather see what he or she thinks is there. Part of the process of internal examination may require a person to identify a good and trusted "proof reader."

One of the challenges that Kim and Sylvester struggle with is providing specific information about the prevalent values and beliefs of certain cultures. If we begin to say that this particular group values and believes thusly and that particular group values and believes something different, then we are perpetuating the use of stereotypes, something that will be discussed in great detail in Chapter 6.

It is important to understand that values are constantly evolving and that there are significant variations in values within each cultural group. In fact, there are probably more differences within a particular cultural group than there are between different groups. So while providing specific information about a culture can be valuable—particularly when dealing with the laws of a particular culture—we must avoid stereotyping and understand that the cultural values, beliefs, and behaviors of each person are individualized. Get to know each person as an individual, rather than as some anonymous member of a certain cultural group.

Values and beliefs are affected by any number of cultural variables including gender, education level, socioeconomic status, employment, religion, sexual orientation, and military status. Our parents play an important role in developing our values and beliefs. Instilling in us a sense of right and wrong is one of their jobs, but did you ever think that this education can potentially be part of the problem of intolerance?

The Role our Caregivers Play

As we are developing and growing, our caregivers, usually our parents, begin to teach us about right and wrong—whether consciously or not. Do you remember some of the messages you received as a child?

- Boys don't cry.
- Tell the truth.
- Be careful; don't get hurt.
- Education is important.
- Don't smoke or use drugs.
- Drinking and driving is bad.
- You can be anything you want to be.
- I hope I never get *that* old—
  his quality of life is awful!
- Don't play with that girl—I don't like her parents.
- There isn't anything you can't do
  if you try hard enough.
- If you hang around people who do bad things,
  you will get the same reputation.

On and on it goes. These were some of the messages that Kim and Sylvester heard as they were growing up. Maybe you heard some of the same messages or perhaps yours were different. As you read these messages, you may think, "These messages sound positive and uplifting to me." Please realize that your assessment is just that . . . YOUR assessment; it may not be shared by everyone else.

Many of the messages that we are exposed to are considered to be words of wisdom. They are reinforced over and over again. The repetition demonstrates the degree of credence given the message. When we hear something frequently and with conviction, we tend to believe that it is true. We then accept this perception of the truth and subconsciously allow it to penetrate the very core of our being. We begin to walk and talk the message. We believe that anyone who believes differently than we do is wrong and that we are right.

Take some time to think about the early messages you received and how they may have shaped the person you've become. What were the messages on religion? Marriage? Education? These early messages are extremely powerful because they come from people we completely trust, people whom we are dependent upon for our very survival. Sometimes we accept their messages without question and incorporate them into the very core fiber of our being. Other times we may completely reject the values and beliefs of our caregivers. But even if we later reject some of the messages taught to us in our formative years, we never forget them. They are always somewhere in our psyche, ready to be regurgitated when the situation arises.

These messages play a major role in our ability to work with others. If my early message was "a day's pay for a day's work", my work ethic will probably be drastically different from someone who received the message that the world owes him or her a living. When you put these two individuals in the same work environment, there is a high likelihood that tension and disagreement will arise.

Mismatched Values

A mismatch occurs when we notice a contradiction between someone's words and their actions, as happens when our mother tells us not to smoke even though she smokes three packs a day. The way she may handle this discrepancy is by letting us know that she realizes smoking is bad for her but it's very difficult for her to stop. She may even get other adults who think like her to reinforce her position. However, in our minds there is still a mismatch.

Another type of mismatch happens when we recognize a discrepancy between what someone says and their reality. This may occur, for example, when our father tells us that the only way to get ahead is through hard work, but we notice that he never gets ahead even though he works long, hard hours. This scenario provides us with an interesting discrepancy. Although we never see our father getting ahead, the value of hard work has been planted. To further complicate the scenario, we may see other people who appear to work very little but have many material things in their life.

Finally, there may be times when we completely reject our caregivers' messages. This may occur, for example, when parents use physical punishment, sometimes adding, "You know, this hurts me more than it does you." That child may vow never to use corporal punishment with his or her own children.

Developing One's Own Value System

Even as all the sifting and sorting of our caregivers' messages is taking place, we start developing our own sense of right and wrong. As young children prior to adolescence, we pretty much mirror the values and beliefs of our parents or primary caregivers. However, during adolescence, as we separate from our parents and become individuals, we start to deviate from the beliefs and values that we were taught. We begin to develop our own sense of right and wrong. This occurs often as a rebellion of our parents' belief system—though we can never be completely void of our parents' influence, since their values and beliefs were implanted in our minds from the time we were born.

Sometimes we may be too frightened or intimidated to express our rebellion out loud to our parents; but we certainly think of our disagreement with their values and possibly share our thoughts with some of our peers. The desire to carry out these hidden thoughts comes from the messages we get from our peer group, which typically are in conflict with the messages we receive from our caregivers. While we may view this as independence, this phase is reactionary and still intimately tied to our parents' values and beliefs.

Sylvester remembers "knowing" that eating sweets before dinner would ruin his appetite. His parents delivered this message to him time and time again. He actually believed it was true, despite the fact that he had never ruined his appetite. His peer group provided a different message. They believed that eating sweets before dinner would actually make their dinner taste better!

As we come to develop our own personal sense of what is right and wrong for us, we may closely mirror our parents' value system. Or we may completely reject everything our parents ever stood for. Most of the time, however, the majority of our values and beliefs are similar to our parents', but with some of our own original thoughts, beliefs, and values sprinkled in.

Righteousness

Developing our own value system is inevitable and proper. While this is a necessary aspect of our development, we may find ourselves moving in the direction of *righteousness.* Once we know what is right and wrong for us, we may take a giant step and assume we now know what is right and wrong for everyone! Righteousness limits our ability to be objective and accepting of others. We tend to view their behaviors and decisions from our own egocentric point of view. If their behaviors don't line up with what we believe to be right, then we label them as wrong.

Do you recognize this position? Everyone has been righteous on at least a few occasions. We certainly have and still, on occasion, catch ourselves doing so. Some of us may not recognize righteousness because righteousness feels completely right to us. This is where objective internal evaluation and your "proof reader" can be of assistance—although we may become so righteous that neither objectivity nor "proof reading" will help!

We all know people who are the epitome of righteousness. Kim has a friend who has strong opinions about almost every topic. She believes everyone should stay abreast of current events or risk being perceived as unintelligent. She has strong opinions that everyone should travel the world, even if they are content in their home towns. She is a liberal democrat who thinks anyone from the political right is stupid or brainwashed. And the list goes on.

When Kim's son bought his first car, she disapproved. When Kim bought her "midlife crisis" sports car, she expressed that Kim wasn't being practical. She has developed the right code for herself and consequently believes that she also has the answers for everyone else. This is where the danger comes in. When we begin to believe that our way is the best way or the only way, we don't leave any room for tolerance, let alone appreciation, of any difference.

Let's say, for example, that you wholeheartedly believe in the value of education. Since it is a strongly held value for the vast majority in this country it becomes easy to believe that it is an absolute universal law. But what about the boy who is 18 and still in the eighth grade? Is finishing high school the best thing for him? Before you answer, consider the fact that he may be attending school with your sons or daughters while in his 20s!

Along these same lines, many parents believe that college is critical to their children's success. Kim has a friend whose daughter struggled through high school with a learning disability. She hated school and had no intention of attending college. She wanted to become a massage therapist. Because her mother wholeheartedly believed in the power of education, she insisted that her daughter attend one year of college. The daughter went but didn't do well and hated every minute of her college experience. She later enrolled in massage school and currently is making more money than her parents.

She is extremely happy and satisfied with her chosen profession. She didn't need college to be successful at all!

Mainstream American Cultural Values

When we ask participants in our training groups to list the underlying values and beliefs of mainstream American culture, they frequently generate a list that looks like this:

- democracy

- individuality

- capitalism

- the Protestant work ethic

- male superiority

- medical model approach to health and wellness

- success measured by socioeconomic status

- linear thinking

- the ends justify the means

- youth valued over experience and old age

Do you recognize these values in American mainstream culture? Do you consider yourself a member of America's mainstream culture? If you do, then would you say that you agree 100% with the aforementioned values? There are ten items. Do they represent your personal value system?

If you don't agree with all of them, do you agree with eight of them? How about six? The point is that while a culture's overall value system can usually be enumerated by its members, often the individual members do not ascribe to all the values of their prevailing cultural group.

Occasionally a major event or disaster will temporarily unite a larger culture filled with many co-cultures. The larger cultural values to which we ascribe tend to become magnified and there is a greater likelihood that we will act on them. We may display the flag. We may wear red, white, and blue. But these overt temporary behaviors are not consistent with our true nature or usual behavior. When the fanfare is over, we revert back to that which is normal and habitual for us.

Sweeping Generalizations

For this reason, it is dangerous to make generalized statements about a particular culture, such as all blacks like fried chicken, all whites are racists, or all Hispanics value extended family. When discussing values and beliefs, remember that they are like opinions. Everyone is entitled to have theirs, and they are neither right nor wrong. They simply represent a person's view of the world.

There has been much speculation surrounding the response to the victims of Hurricane Katrina. Many have said that race was the primary reason for the delay in assistance. Others have stated other reasons, such as the military's involvement in Iraq, lack of an effective emergency response plan, and the socioeconomic status of the victims.

Our view of the world and everything in it is the primary motivation for all of our responses. The lens through which we see may have a different focus than that of other people. Therefore, our reaction to a particular person, situation, or part of the world may be different than what others would expect.

Just this week, we were speaking with a Puerto Rican woman who is married to a Vietnamese man. She shared that his family did not readily accept her because they believed that all Hispanics are lazy. This woman had to prove herself against a stereotype before her in-laws would accept her into their family. Although she experienced some resistance in the beginning, she was able to finally be accepted because she had an advocate—her husband.

If you have a connection to someone from a different culture, there is a greater chance that you will be accepted. There is also the chance that the person bringing you into the culture may lose some of the respect of his or her peers. Sylvester knew of a young black boy who was labeled an "Uncle Tom" by his peers because he spoke a certain way and was openly accepted by a racially integrated upper class student group.

Expanding Beyond Righteousness

If you are going down the path of honoring and respecting diversity, the first step you must take is to examine your own values and beliefs. Leave your righteousness on the early part of the path; it will not serve you in this quest.

Another word for this type of righteousness is ethnocentrism. Ethnocentrism creates a group's, and consequently an individual's, righteousness. Ethnocentrism causes individuals to view the world from their own culture, and then assume that their culture is better than others. Anytime you start to believe that your way is the best and only way for everyone, you have entered dangerous territory. In subsequent chapters we will explain how ethnocentrism begins the cycle of prejudice and oppression.

Just because people believe, value, or do things differently than you do, doesn't mean that they are wrong. It simply means that they are different. In this difference there may be something for you to learn. A different perspective or opinion may provide the seeds for an answer to a problem you are experiencing.

We often encourage people to listen to a different type of music, or watch a different type of television program, than they typically do so that they can experience the flavor and the value of something other than their norm. People develop their personal tastes and then avoid anything different from what they like; this results in a limited view of the world. If they were to sample other cultures, they might find a large part of society that they never knew existed.

Though we all respect knowledge, there are times when our right-eousness will prohibit us from gaining the knowledge we need to become more accepting of other cultures. Opening ourselves up, instead of shutting down to difference, can greatly expand our pool of knowledge and resources, making us all more effective.

In the next chapter, we will discuss the myths that begin the cycle of prejudice and oppression.

Myths

Much of the intolerance we have for diversity and differences is fueled by early childhood messages we received about others who were different from us.

How Myths Develop

As infants, our main concern is our own survival. As we mature and grow, we become aware of our familiar primary caregivers. Provided we received adequate care, we begin to expand our circle of influence to include our immediate family members as well. Over time we expand even further to include our friends and community.

As adults we generally feel safest and most comfortable with people who are familiar and most like us. Our comfort zone lies in relationships with people with whom we share something in common. Our comfort zone may be organized around our own gender, race, religion, occupation, hobbies, or any other co-culture to which we may belong. This is where we feel most comfortable and accepted. In order to stay at this level of comfort and acceptance, we will sometimes avoid other cultures.

We generally have an aversion, or at least initially a mistrust, of others whom we view as "different" in some way. This mistrust can grow into fear if we do not take active steps to increase our knowledge and experience of that person. Fear fuels the myths, misinformation, and possibly even outright lies about a particular target group. These myths are spoken aloud, learned, and passed onto others. They spread like a big juicy tidbit of gossip!

Most myths about a group actually begin without any direct experience of that group whatsoever. In fact, in order for myths to be perpetuated, a certain amount of distance and objectification of the target group is required. Myths are based on perceptual fact. When we actually get to know a group of people, we will often have experiences that are in direct conflict with the myths that we have heard and come to believe. Because of this possibility, when we are taught myths about a group we are also often encouraged to stay away from it.

Myths may be based on hearsay, television, the movies, or the person's own active imagination. If the myth is based on an actual experience, it is typically a very limited experience. For example, a person you know may have been robbed by a person with black skin; the myth then becomes that all blacks are dangerous criminals. When we allow ourselves to subscribe to these general beliefs based on isolated incidents, we are closing our minds and are no longer objective.

The topic of disproportionality is beyond the scope of this book, but stated simply disproportionality occurs when the system set up by the powerful majority culture creates rules, schemes, and institutions that unfairly oppress and punish the minority cultures. The system then uses this fact—for example, that more people of color are in jails, special education programs, and on welfare—to perpetuate myths that people of color are criminals, stupid, and lazy. Disproportionality is another reality that supports the perpetuation of myths.

Early Childhood Messages

If someone were to ask you to identify early childhood messages that you received about particular groups, you would have little difficulty recalling them. Let's give it a try. Clear your mind and allow the first thought that comes up to take shape in response to the question. Don't try to censor your thoughts. Whether you agree with the messages or not, allow yourself to remember them.

What did you hear as a child regarding old people? How about Jewish people? Hispanics? Asians? African-Americans? Caucasians? Native

Americans? Bi-racial individuals? What about gays, lesbians, and bisexuals? What were you told about people from the country? People from the city? People whose first language is not English? Alcoholics and/or drug addicts? Homeless people? Middle Easterners? Muslims? Welfare recipients? People with disabilities? Poor people? Wealthy people? Men? Women? The list is endless.

Part of the human condition is to somehow make sense of the world by organizing our information and experiences. This is what we are genetically programmed to do. This tendency serves us well when we are learning about hot stoves, electrical outlets, and playing in the street. However it is a disservice when we attempt to categorize people.

Were you able to call up your early messages? Kim will now share some of her early messages with you:

- Old people are just in the way—slow and terrible drivers.

- Poor people are lazy and do nothing to help themselves.

- Jewish people ban together and are cheap.

- Hispanics are lazy and sleep in the middle of the day.

- Asians are very smart and good in math and with computers.

- African-Americans are scary and angry

- Native Americans, poor things, are all alcoholics and very poor.

- Bi-racial people have a difficult life but it isn't their fault—their parents never should have made a child together.

- People whose first language is not English should go back to where they came from or learn our language.

- Stay away from alcoholics and drug addicts—they are dangerous and can hurt you!

Here are some of Sylvester's early messages:

- Whites are not to be trusted.

- Whites are always out to hurt or do something against blacks and you should not cavort with them.

- Don't you ever bring a white woman to this house!

- Blacks should be with blacks and whites should be with whites.

- We are Christians and follow Jesus.

- Homosexuality is wrong.

Actually, Kim doesn't even remember her parents discussing homosexuality, probably because for her parents, gays and lesbians didn't exist. Although there are groups that exist and are not liked, an early message may be to not acknowledge them. While Kim's parents chose avoidance in dealing with homosexuality, Sylvester remembers being told that homosexuality was just wrong; God made Adam and Eve, not Adam and Steve!

Kim heard nothing about Caucasians because she belonged to that group. Being from the country, she didn't hear things about country folks either—but people from the city were terrible drivers. Although Kim heard nothing about Middle Easterners when she was growing up, she believes, with the stigma that exists since 9/11, many children today do.

Muslims were not discussed in her house either, nor were welfare recipients. Kim was always told not to stare at people with disabilities. She heard that wealthy people were stingy and full of themselves. She was raised to believe that women should be subservient to their husbands and take care of the children, while the man's job was to make a good living and provide for his family.

Sylvester recalls that the majority of his early childhood messages were against the dominant white culture.

Just recalling these early messages was almost like therapy. Do Kim. and Sylvester believe any of these myths today? They would like to say no. However, whether they believe in them or not, they are still inside of them. The danger with early messages is that they stick with you. You may not act on them and you may not believe them, but as long as they are inside you, there is a danger of recall. Kim and Sylvester were able to call them up without any difficulty. The fact that they have rejected some of the myths they were taught as children doesn't mean that they have forgotten what they are.

Myths Lead to Stereotyping

What is the problem with myths and why are they so destructive? Myths lead to stereotyping, which is the subject of the next chapter. This is an area that is not discussed much when we talk about human relationships. When we talk about injustices and oppression we hear words such as prejudice, discrimination, and racism. But the belief in myths is what is really at the root of all of these issues.

When we are fed myths about a certain group of people, we come to believe the myths as truth. However, there is never a statement about a group of people that is **always** true for every single member of that group. Of course there are cultural trends, and it's helpful to be aware of them when interacting with people of a different culture. Kim and Sylvester are careful about the time they spend on cultural trends because there are some who will use this information to form stereotypes rather than spend time to get to know the individuals involved.

When you begin to believe you know something about an individual based upon these myths, you are forming prejudicial opinions about a person before you even know him or her, and run the risk of being completely wrong.

Myths are Told to Us by Those We Trust

One of the big problems with early childhood messages is that we hear them from people and institutions that we trust. Who is it that gave you your early childhood messages? Kim received hers from her parents, grandparents, the church, and teachers. These are all people and institutions that we expect will tell us the truth.

It is difficult to admit, even today, that the people we trusted gave us inaccurate information. We don't like to feel that we are compromising our culture, something we will discuss in Chapter 13. Kim's father was very upset when she came home from her fourth grade class one day to tell him she had learned that porcupines throw their quills. Her father knew this was a myth and wanted to make sure Kim understood that. Kim adored her teacher and had a hard time believing that she was wrong. However, ultimately Kim's allegiance was with her father; she accepted his word as truth. Being caught in such a "mythical conflict" can be good. Having two or more people whom you love and respect give you conflicting information may encourage you to do further research to determine the truth for yourself.

Kim also remembers the day she learned that the myths her parents had been feeding her during her childhood—about Santa Claus, the tooth fairy and the Easter bunny—were untrue. She was devastated, not because these characters that she had grown to love did not really exist, but because her parents had lied to her. Many adults don't think about the effect that their lying will have on their children when the truth finally comes out.

Well-meaning parents such as Kim's tell these myths to enhance the experience of childhood. Kim's parents never meant to hurt her; they were only passing along myths that they were given. Most parents in the United States have told these myths to their children, consciously knowing that they are not true. But how many other myths have well-meaning parents been sharing unconsciously?

The myths that begin stereotyping are typically not deliberate lies.

Most people who provided your early messages actually believed their veracity. They were telling you their version of life as total truth. When you share with others a myth that you believe is true, you are doing it to help them. You want to prepare them for their journey through life. When you have that level of sincerity in your heart, your message comes across genuinely and heartfelt. How can children not believe these messages from people whom they love and trust?

Recognizing and Dispelling Myths

We need to become aware of the myths we have learned and be vigilant about not passing them on to the young people who trust us and look to us for guidance. This can be challenging because it means that we are doubting, to some degree, what we were taught. We may feel that we are betraying the people who provided us with the information. However relying on our own direct experience, rather than other's teachings, is liberation, not betrayal.

In business, there are many myths that can circulate; if we are not careful, these can cause division within the workplace. Sylvester recalls a time when he worked with a group of people who believed that working with Christians was boring because they didn't know how to have fun. Although he had grown up in a Christian home, he had never worked with Christians. His experience from church was that Christians were people who prayed, sang, and believed in following the Ten Commandments.

When Sylvester had an opportunity to work with a new co-worker of the Christian faith, he believed she would be boring and would make his life miserable at work. However, after working a few weeks with his new co-worker, he realized that there were things about her that did not line up with the information he had received. As he got to know this young woman, he became fond of her. They laughed and joked a lot and eventually became good friends. Oftentimes our perception of the myths that we were given is greatly altered by our direct experience.

Myths in the Workplace

Not all myths develop during our early childhood. One of the most common occurrences in the workplace is the sharing of myths. There is always someone who has formed a myth about another employee. Usually most employees have a perception about the supervisor. Although they believe that the information they are offering is accurate, it may not be accurate for you.

Many times co-workers believe that they are giving you information to make your transition smoother; in fact what they are really doing is limiting your opportunity to develop a genuine point of view. Most people will give you their impression of a person, or a group of people, based on their own experience. They may tell you that the managers in the company are tyrants. They may tell you that this company is run like a dictatorship. They may even share with you an incident that occurred to further substantiate their claims. But part of the story may be missing, such as what precipitated the behavior of the manager.

The manager may be nothing like the mythical description you have been given. You must decide whether you are going to believe in the myth or in your actual experience. Your actual experience may totally contradict the myth. Do not deny your own experience, even if the myth comes from a source perceived to be reliable.

To decrease the possibility that myths will affect the relationships within your organization, you can create an atmosphere where the employees are given the opportunity to socialize and relate to each other. Co-workers can have luncheons together. Regular discussions can be facilitated that will allow employees the opportunity to get to know each other without myths.

Myths are a consistent influence in our quest to get to know people. Although they can be detrimental, they provide us with a feeling of comfort when we encounter certain groups, because we think we know them. This feeling lulls us into a false sense of security. Know that all information we receive is only someone's opinion. Take time to check things out for yourself. Your own personal knowledge can enhance your awareness and create a high level of cultural sensitivity.

Myths lead to stereotyping. The next chapter will discuss what stereotypes are and how to minimize their use.

Stereotypes

The myths, misinformation, and missing information that we experience give rise to stereotypes. Stereotypes are generalizations representing an over-simplified opinion, attitude, or judgment concerning a person or group. Stereotypes can be based on a cultural norm which has been distorted or carried to extremes, or they can be based on a total misunderstanding of the group or culture.

When stereotypes are reinforced by our families, communities, and the media, they become credible. We begin to internalize this information and the myths become our truths. Once internalized, even members of the target group may begin to believe the stereotype of their group. This can have a huge impact on their identity development, resulting in self-doubt, low self-esteem, and minimal expectations for their future.

Jane Elliott's Phenomenal Exercise

Never was the effect of stereotyping more obvious than in Jane Elliott's exercise called, "Blue Eyes, Brown Eyes."[1] Ms. Elliott was a school teacher in Riceville, Iowa during the 1960s. After the assassination of Dr. Martin Luther King, Jr., Ms. Elliott decided it was time to show her students, in a very real way, what people of color experience in the United States—by starting an exercise.

On the first day, she told her students that blue-eyed people were smarter than brown-eyed people. In addition, they had better manners, told the truth more, and got better grades in school. On the other hand, brown-eyed people were greedy and couldn't be trusted.

Since Ms. Elliot had a good relationship with her students, they were inclined to believe anything she said.

The results were amazing! These students, who had cooperated with each other prior to receiving this misinformation, turned into vicious, discriminating third graders. The class quickly became divided around eye color. In order to make it clear who had the darker eyes, Ms. Elliott made the brown-eyed students wear blue felt collars around their necks so that they could be recognized easily. Throughout the day, she would accentuate the positive behavior of the students who weren't wearing the collars, while she would be quick to point out when a child with a collar made a mistake or misbehaved.

To be fair, Ms. Elliott switched the situation around on the second day, making the blue-eyed children wear the collar. She told the children that she had lied to them the day before; it was really brown-eyed children who were smarter and better behaved than blue-eyed children.

Jane Elliott's exercise will be discussed further in subsequent chapters. What's important to understand at this point is how easy it was for a trusted person to feed third graders misinformation and then have them not only believe it, but also act viciously upon it.

Just as in Ms. Elliott's exercise, the real world provides misinformation all the time. Kim knew a man in her town who hated black people. He had, admittedly, never even met a black man. All he knew was what a friend of his, a racist New York City police officer, had told him. Never having any of his own experiences, the person Kim knew chose to believe his trusted friend, whom he viewed as an authority on the subject. He came to believe that all black men were criminals and couldn't be trusted.

There are so many stereotypes based upon total fiction. One is that blacks are not as smart as whites, which is as ridiculous as the blue eyes, brown eyes discrimination. We need to realize that the disproportionality that exists in our social, educational, and legal systems affects socioeconomic status more than anything else. This argument was masterfully discussed in Dr. Ruby Payne's book, *A Framework for Understanding Poverty.*[2]

Disproportionality

More people of color live in poverty in this country than white people. The quality of education in lower income areas is inferior to that of the more affluent areas, due to the lower tax base. Teachers are underpaid and lack the resources available in more affluent districts; therefore, the quality of education tends to be inferior. Furthermore, people who live in lower economic areas are generally not exposed to the same life experiences as people in the upper economic strata.

The intelligence testing performed in most school systems has been shown to be culturally biased, with questions favoring the majority culture rather than the minority cultures.

Disproportionality can be traced back to root causes that have nothing to do with skin color. What would happen if you took an affluent college educated couple, stripped them of their degrees, placed them in a low-income housing area, and took away their jobs and cars from them? You might say that they would fight to regain their status, using all the resources available to them. This might be true given the fact that they had the experience of knowing what is possible. But what if they never had the degrees or the jobs? What if they never lived in a nice area or never had cars? What would be their recourse then?

Can Stereotypes be Positive?

Some stereotypes are positive; or are they? What about the stereotype that all Asians are good in math and technology? Or that blacks are good in sports? How about Latinos are good lovers? Even though these stereotypes seem to be saying something positive about a group of people, there is something inherently wrong with these statements.

First of all, they are not true. Not *all* Asians are good in math and technology. Not *all* blacks are good in sports. Not *all* Latinos are good lovers. Since there are exceptions, the stereotype is nothing more than a broad generalization about a group of people that can't possibly be true for every member in it.

Secondly, imagine what it feels like to be the exception to the rule. What would it be like to be the one Asian with a C in math, or the one black who is uncoordinated and can't play sports, or the one Latino who is shy and has had no sexual experience? These so-called positive stereotypes are deadly for them. The people not fitting the stereotype could be racked with self-esteem issues because they can't live up to the expectations.

Finally, these "positive" stereotypes can pigeonhole people and not allow them to live up to their potential. Imagine the Asian worker who was hired for his technological skills. He is a computer genius and is going a great job. However, his goal is to become a manager in the customer service department. Even though he may have terrific managerial skills as well, he may never get the chance to demonstrate them because management believes that he belongs in his current job.

Stereotypes can overlook a person's true strengths. Kim has an African-American friend named Debbie, who has a son the same age as Kim's older son. Kim's son was accepted at Indiana University of Pennsylvania in their marketing program. Debbie's son was accepted into Penn State's engineering program, with a full academic scholarship. Whenever Kim or Debbie were asked what their children were doing, they would respond by saying that their children were entering their first year of college. The follow up question Kim would be asked is, "What's your son's major?" Debbie often mentioned that her son had a scholarship, because she was very proud of that fact. The follow up question she would be asked is, "What sport does he play?" No one meant any harm by that question, but the "positive" stereotype presumed that her son's scholarship had to be athletic rather than academic.

So is the stereotype positive? No, never. No stereotype is ever positive, nor is it ever true. A stereotype, by its very definition, presupposes something about a person based upon their membership within a particular group. No stereotype is ever true for every member of a group.

Stereotypes are Not True

So, why do we do it? Why do we stereotype? It is our way of categorizing people so that we can convince ourselves that we know something about them. While categorizing objects is acceptable, categorizing people can be extremely hurtful. Instead of taking the time to get to know individuals, we stereotype them so that we feel as though we know something about them, even though we don't. What we have done, in fact, is placed a wall between us that will prohibit us from ever knowing them.

Another friend of Kim's, Nancy, travels a great deal by plane. During one trip, Nancy flew through the Philadelphia airport and had a negative experience with some people there who, according to her, were being rude. As Nancy shared this story with her children and some acquaintances, they unanimously agreed, "That's right. Don't you know that all people in Philadelphia are mean?" Kim learned of Nancy's stereotype when she informed Nancy that she was considering moving to Philadelphia. Nancy advised, "Oh, don't move there. Everyone in Philly is mean."

Fortunately, Kim had had direct experiences which disputed this stereotype. Otherwise she may have fallen prey to believing it and would have stayed away from Philadelphia at all costs. People like Nancy who make blanket statements are fairly comfortable in their position until they are challenged. When challenged they may acquiesce to some degree; however, they usually continue believing the stereotype that has taken root in their hearts. In Nancy's case it was, "All Philadelphians are mean."

Another person Kim knows, Patty, spent three days in Chicago and experienced horrendous traffic the entire time she was there. Ever since that trip, Patty has been telling anyone who will listen, "Don't ever go to Chicago. All you will do is sit for hours in traffic." Now, Kim happens to live in Chicago and she knows that there is a traffic problem. But it does not exist every minute of every day as Patty adamantly informs anyone she knows who is considering traveling to Chicago.

Another woman Kim knows returned from Italy claiming that all Italian women are beautiful. Kim incredulously asked, "*All* of them?" And the traveler swore that yes, there was not one unattractive Italian woman in all of Italy!

Some of these stereotypes may seem quite innocuous. However, many stereotypes border on criminal. We've heard stereotypes claiming that certain groups of people are stupid, lazy, dangerous, smelly, promiscuous, and drug users. None of these stereotypes seem innocuous to us.

Many Stereotypes Have Some Basis in Reality

One of the challenges is that many stereotypes are based, in part, on cultural norms and trends. The stereotype that blacks like to play basketball may be based on the number of African-Americans who are playing basketball in the streets. If you think about the fact that the average African-American lives in the city, what sport is available to city dwellers? Basketball courts exist all around the city. It is rare to see a football field in the middle of an urban neighborhood. Could these two factors—living in the city and playing basketball—be related?

There are many stereotypes that exist about females: that they are overemotional and illogical in their decision-making; that they are passive and nonassertive; that they are family-oriented and not seriously committed to their careers. While some of these stereotypes may have been born out of some degree of truth, they are not true for every woman.

A common stereotype of blacks is that they have rhythm. When Sylvester, Kim, and her son were on the driving range in Kim's rural hometown, they encountered an older white male practicing his drive. Kim and Sylvester had finished hitting their balls and decided to take a break to have a Coke. Kim's son and the older gentleman continued to hit their golf balls. When they were finished they came over to us, and the older gentleman began to tell us about Kim's son's swing. He said that her son had a lot of power, that he hit the ball straight, but the only thing he was missing was rhythm. Then, he turned to Sylvester, looked him directly in the eye and said, "And you should teach him that!"

Everything that Sylvester had learned, up until that point in his life, told him that he should retaliate, so that this man would understand that he can't get away with stereotypes like that. Instead, Sylvester looked at him and said, "Yes, I do have rhythm." This man's comment may have angered other black people, but for Sylvester it showed just how isolated and out of touch the man really was. He lived in a very rural part of Pennsylvania and he may never have encountered any other black people in his lifetime. In hindsight, Sylvester thinks that the man was probably attempting to connect with him in his own way. Sylvester does not believe that this man was being mean and malicious; but he does believe that the man was operating from a very narrow perspective, resulting from a life of stereotyping.

The Value of Understanding
Cultural Trends and Tendencies

When we are working in a diverse environment, it is helpful to be aware of cultural trends and tendencies. Some cultural trends may revolve around personal space, physical touching, eye contact, etc. Of course, anything that can be said of these trends—such as how much personal space a person from a certain culture requires—will be a stereotype and therefore not always true for every member of a cultural group. However, a description of general tendencies can provide some information to a person who is interacting with different cultural groups.

Kim was working with some black evacuees from Hurricane Katrina who had truly experienced culture shock—coming from New Orleans to a white, affluent, urban setting. One of Kim's co-workers was taking issue with an evacuee who was allowing other residents to discipline her children. In the co-worker's culture, no one would dare correct her children while she was in their presence. However, in the culture of southern blacks, this custom is not uncommon. The co-worker did not understand the cultural norms of the evacuees and consequently placed a negative value on this young mother's behavior.

The Damage of Stereotyping in the Workplace

Stereotypes can make it impossible for relationships within an organization to develop. Coming into a company can be frightening. There are new rules to learn, new people to meet, and new responsibilities that lie ahead. New employees do their best: they take care of their appearance; they are on time; they work above and beyond the call of duty. Yet, they may not be respected or accepted by their peers because of stereotypes. This becomes frustrating for the new employees; they begin to slack off. Why should they work so hard when it is not being appreciated? Why should they come in early and stay late when their efforts are not being recognized?

Let's say that the new employee is a woman. She is working in a company that is predominantly staffed by males. Upon hearing that a woman is coming to work with them, the stereotypes began to fly. "She's not going to be able to carry her weight." "She is going to be emotional and moody." "She is only going to slow us down because she is weak." Although the woman is nothing like this, the men will not let go of their stereotypes easily. These stereotypes help them feel knowledgeable about her, without taking the time to get to know her. They believed they knew her when she walked through the door!

After weeks of working hard without being recognized, the woman stops trying. She believes that men will never recognize a woman, so why bother? In the end, the relationship between the woman and her male co-workers never develops because both sides are using stereotypes.

Stereotypes are dangerous and can totally destroy relationships. We often don't recognize them because they are born out of our ethnocentrism and are taught by people whom we know and trust. While it is very difficult to prevent people from stereotyping, we can bring it to a conscious level so that we will recognize it when it happens.

In the next chapter, we will discuss how stereotyping leads to prejudice.

Prejudice

"Prejudice is an emotional commitment to ignorance."
—Nathan Rutstein

Once stereotyping becomes entrenched, prejudice begins. Prejudice is defined as a bias—an opinion, often unfavorable, formed without adequate reasons. Prejudice refers to values, beliefs, and opinions held toward a particular group of people. It typically results in a negative attitude toward unknown people based simply upon their association with a target group.

Prejudice can be strongly present in all groups; it does not require having power, as oppression does. Oppression will be discussed further in the next chapter, but the bottom line is that in order for one group to oppress another, the oppressing group must have power over the group being oppressed.

Prejudice, however, can be present in the group that is being oppressed, as well as in the group doing the oppressing. Prejudice exists anytime one person judges or forms an opinion about another person, not personally known to him or her, based on membership in a particular group. Whites can be prejudiced towards blacks, just as blacks can be prejudiced towards whites. Heterosexuals can be prejudiced towards homosexuals in the same way that homosexuals can hold prejudicial feelings against heterosexuals. Older people can be prejudiced against young people, just as young people can be prejudiced against the elderly.

A Case of Negative Bias

Kim was an excellent student in school. Getting good grades was important to her and doing so was fairly easy. During her undergraduate studies in psychology, she took an elective called "Personality," a class about personality development. Guess what happened? Kim flunked Personality. That's right! She got a big, fat "F" on her college transcript in the area of personality. Do you know how hard it is to explain that the "F" existed because of an extreme case of prejudice on the part of one of her Caucasian professors?

Here is the story that she swears is true. On the first day of class, her professor called Kim to his desk and said to her, "Miss Daub (Kim's maiden name), I suggest you drop my class. You will not pass. You have the same hostile look on your face that my son has."

Imagine Kim's surprise! She had never done anything to this man. She certainly wasn't feeling hostile and she had never met his son. She also knew that she would never fail a course. She had never received anything less than a B in her entire life! Needless to say, she stubbornly stayed in the class, determined to prove her worth through hard work, intelligence, and determination. She persevered. Every test was an essay exam. Normally very good at essay tests, Kim was repeatedly surprised when her tests came back with red Fs marked on them. She knew she had adequately covered the material. There were other students with better grades who had far less information on their exams. What was wrong?

For the first time in her life, Kim experienced prejudice. This professor had formed an erroneous opinion about her, based on her apparent likeness to his son. There was no way she could get a fair deal in this professor's class. Just so you know the rest of the story, she repeated the class the next semester with a different professor and received an A.

This is just one example of the many forms that prejudice can take— being negative without cause.

A Case of Positive Bias

Another example of prejudice is the reverse—being positive without a basis in reality. Sylvester is an assistant coach of a boy's basketball team. In the two years that he has been involved with the boys, he has noticed an interesting phenomenon: most of the parents are prejudiced in this way.

There was one instance when a new parent introduced himself and his son to the coaches. He raved about his son's playing ability and said he looked forward to attending the games. When the season began, the father noticed that his son was not a starter on the team and he was not happy with this decision. However, when he looked at the talent on the team, he seemed to understand. He attended the first few practices and could clearly see that his son was not comfortable on the court. After practice, he would talk to his son about his fears and his comfort level. His son would reply that everything was fine, and that would be the end of the conversation.

After several games, the father walked up to Sylvester and said, "What did you do to my son?" What the parent was implying was that the coaching staff had somehow affected his son's playing ability, and his son no longer was as good as he used to be. It was clear to Sylvester that this father had a bias toward his son. Whenever we have biases, it becomes difficult for us to see objectively and make decisions based on reality.

This example of prejudice based on a positive bias is the one form of prejudice that many people believe does no harm. Personal biases are normal. Naturally, you are going to prefer some things over others. This is how we are made. Can you imagine a world where everyone likes all things equally? It would be incredibly boring! However, trouble begins when these biases cloud our ability to see things objectively. Consequently we engage in judging or scrutinizing others when it may be inappropriate to do so, as when the father unfairly criticized the coaching staff for his son's mediocre performance.

In business, there will always be employees who outshine and out-work others. We often use terms like "go-getter" or "driven" to describe these employees who take initiative and get the job done. These are the employees who understand the goals of the team and who go above and beyond the call of duty to accomplish these goals. A successful coach or manager will identify his outstanding players early on and will lean heavily on them for performance. However, coaches and managers must also remain objective enough to know when their star players are not playing their best. Everyone has a bad day, and if managers don't realize or accept this, their bias can put the company in jeopardy.

In baseball, teams rely on relief pitchers. While there are starting pitchers who begin the game, relief pitchers back them up if the starters are not playing up to par. The team is hopeful that their starters can finish the game. They believe that these pitchers have what it takes to go the distance. But if for some reason the starting pitcher does not perform at an optimal level, the manager may go to the bullpen to call for a relief pitcher. Managers who allow their prejudices to affect their decision-making may never go to the bull-pen, or they may wait too long and go there when it is too late.

The Problems with Prejudice

As managers, it is critical that we recognize reality and are not guided or influenced by our prejudices. Prejudices based on positive bias are strongly encouraged by our allegiance to a person or a group. Naturally, we believe that the individuals we are supporting are the ones who deserve the opportunity and they are the ones for whom we root. Preferring a certain person is generally not a problem unless it prevents someone more qualified from having the position.

A more negative form of prejudice—which comes from our stereo-typical thinking—is based on fear, dislike, or lack of trust,. This form of prejudice will drive a wedge between individuals. In the early 20th century, the prejudices held against women and people of color were derived from the stereotypes that the majority culture strongly held. If you believed that women and people of color were incapable of managing particular tasks or professions, you would prefer to have a white man carry out the responsibility.

For years it was believed that women were not capable of responsibilities that required physical strength. Women were denied many opportunities because they were considered to be physically weaker, and therefore incapable of fulfilling the responsibility of the position. In addition to their perceived physical dominance, men were perceived to be smarter and more intellectual. Women were not encouraged to achieve academically and in many cases were not afforded the opportunity to attend certain educational institutions.

Oftentimes this lack of trust in an individual's ability is accompanied by a lack of respect. Sexual harassment is a legal term, created for the purpose of ending harassment and discrimination against women in the workplace. Although this behavior is not exclusive to women, the majority of the cases filed are cases where a man is the perpetrator and a woman is the victim. This is because in order for harassment to occur, the person accused must be in a position of power over the person being harassed.

Many stereotypes of people of color have led to feelings of fear or dislike. There is a belief that blacks are angry or quick tempered, which has influenced many people to be fearful of them. In the workplace, if you have a problem with someone, it is important that you know you can go to that individual to rectify the situation. If you are afraid of that person's response, you may take your concern to someone else. While this may be more comfortable, you will have failed to address the issue appropriately because of your fear. Allowing your prejudices to dictate your actions can be detrimental to your growth.

As managers and supervisors, you are always called upon to make crucial decisions. Many of these decisions can influence the growth and direction of your company, so making the best decision possible is important. Prejudice may influence you to make ineffective decisions, even if the results do not manifest immediately.

Suppose you, as a manager, have an issue that needs to be addressed with a female on your team. You may hesitate to bring it up because you are concerned that she will become emotional, or that she will think she is being singled out because of her gender. After due consideration, you decide it's not worth the hassle to bring it up. It would appear that you've saved yourself some controversy in the short run and saved your employee some discomfort. However, in the long run, you have deprived one of your employees of the information she needs to take corrective action. Later, when a promotion becomes available, she may be overlooked because there are problems that have never been addressed. This is part of the reason women and other minorities are passed over for promotion.

A Case of Public Prejudice Against Women

In 1973, Bobby Riggs, a former tennis champion, boosted that he could beat the current women's champion, Billie Jean King. Mr. Riggs suggested that Ms. King would never defeat him in a tennis match because of his masculine superiority. Although Riggs was 55 years old at the time, he stated that a woman could never defeat a man because women were simply "too weak." This was a sore spot with Billie Jean King and other women professional sports players. There was clearly an inequity in compensation, as female professional athletes were being paid much less than men. Ms. King had won 20 titles at Wimbledon and organized the Women's Tennis Association, a union of female players that improved their bargaining position. King became the first woman to make more than $100,000 a year in tennis. She was the Associated Press' Woman Athlete of the Year in 1967 and 1973. She was Sports Illustrated's Sportswoman of the Year in 1972. She was Time Magazine's Woman of the Year in 1976. Not just a sportswoman—the all around woman!

When they played the match, Riggs quickly realized that this was going to be a challenge for him even though he was playing against an "inferior" opponent. The match ended with Riggs losing and saying, "She was too good, too fast." For many, this match shifted the way they saw women in the world of sports. It provided a public forum for women to showcase one of their very own, demonstrating superiority over a male.

This match provided a clear example of how we can sometimes allow our prejudices to blind us. Riggs never took his age (55) or his physical ability into account because of his prejudice towards women. His confidence was based on gender, not ability. Had Riggs been able to see King as a great tennis player and not just as a female, he may not have taken her for granted and he may not have boasted that he could win.

How to Minimize Prejudice in the Workplace
Companies all over the world are faced with the challenge of overcoming prejudice in the workplace. Implementing formal systems to deal with, challenge and manage prejudicial thinking and actions is an effective way to minimize these acts of prejudice.

Scheduling discussions concerning issues surrounding prejudice is one way to handle the topic. Many companies hold discussions surrounding current events. A manager can take the responsibility of choosing the topics for discussion and can facilitate the dialogue. This will allow employees to express their opinions and hear the opinions of others. It is important that the manager be objective and in control of his or her own prejudices.

Be sure that before you have any discussions, the group is engaged in the establishment of ground rules. These rules must be put into place to ensure that the discussions run smoothly. The object of the discussions is to open the minds of the employees so that they can learn about the prejudices they carry. Providing lunch at these sessions is always a good idea, as it provides an incentive for involvement and a social forum in which different cultural groups can interact comfortably.

Another way to minimize prejudice in the workplace is to allow individuals to share experiences when they have felt prejudice directed at them, as well as when they have felt prejudiced against someone.

When Prejudice Appears as Consideration

In a training some years ago, a woman shared how she felt underutilized and overlooked because her supervisor never relied on her to perform many of the tasks that men were expected to perform. Although many of these tasks were physical in nature, she wanted to be recognized as a person who could be trusted to carry them out.

She talked about an incident when she and three of her male co-workers were given a task which involved them working in less than favorable conditions. The room did not have heat. They were going to be loading boxes and moving them to another room for storage. As they were discussing how to carry out this task, she noticed that the men were not including her in this preplanning conversation. When she asked about her role, they stated that she could make sure that the boxes were placed in the right section of the storage room. When she responded that she would like to work with them in the basement so that they could get the job done sooner, she was told that it was too cold down there and that packing and carrying the boxes was going to be difficult.

Although she was not looking forward to working in the cold, she wanted to meet the challenge in order to address the prejudice. As she continued to share her story, one gentleman in the room was in shock. He could not understand why she didn't see that these men were just trying to be gentlemen. They just wanted to give her the opportunity to work in a better environment, and he didn't see anything wrong with that.

When she completed her story, he shared that he was a supervisor who had several women working for him. He treated them the same way but believed that he was doing it out of respect for their gender, not prejudice. He believed that women were precious and fragile beings and should not be expected to take on too much. He considered his actions to be sensitive to women; hearing a woman state that these same actions offended her was quite shocking to him.

Oftentimes, the person who is experiencing the prejudice will not recognize it as such. As a result, the person displaying the prejudiced behavior believes that he has acted in good faith. His prejudice becomes reinforced, making it likely that the act will occur again. Had this supervisor not been exposed to this information in training, he would never have known that his perceived acts of kindness were based on prejudice.

It is important that we understand and know where our prejudices lie. We all have prejudices, but when we know and understand them, we have a better chance of managing them. We may not be able to overcome them instantly, since it has taken many years to establish them. But having knowledge of them is a major step.

The next chapter will explain how prejudice often leads to discrimination and oppression.

Discrimination and Oppression

*T*he *New American Webster Handy College Dictionary* (third edition)[1] defines discriminating as

1. judging (the respective merits) or
2. treating differently on the basis of race, class, sex, etc.

For the purposes of this book, the second definition of discrimination will be used: to treat differently on the basis of race, class, sex, etc.

Oppression is defined as treating tyrannically. It is more institutional than discrimination, referring to the substandard and unfair treatment of a target group by the group in power. For oppression to exist, prejudice must be combined with power that is institutional and systemic.

Oppression thrives because the group in power believes that it is superior and has the right, and even the responsibility, to control others. This asserted right is institutionalized; the power group builds its systems around it, ensuring the unfair treatment of the target group. When implementing a full scale diversity initiative at work, employees must develop a personal awareness of the oppression that pervades our society and has been part of our history.

In the next chapter we will discuss at length the concept of "majority privilege." For now, suffice it to say that those in power enjoy certain privileges not afforded to those outside their group. If you are a member of the white majority in this country, can you even imagine what it would be like to be discriminated against because of your skin color?

Discrimination and Oppression in Third Grade

In Jane Elliott's blue eyes/brown eyes exercise, first discussed in Chapter 6, third grade students began oppressing their classmates upon receiving misinformation about them. When Ms. Elliott defined which students would be in power on a particular day, the blue-eyed or the brown-eyed—she set up the ideal scenario for discrimination and oppression to occur.

Once their teacher, whom these third-graders trusted and respected, told them that there were character defects in the group that was "on the bottom" for that day, the group in power began to treat the "defective" group very differently. Children who were previously friends began to taunt each other. The children "on top" wouldn't speak to the children "on the bottom" when outside on the playground.

Ms. Elliott had set it up so that the children in power enjoyed certain privileges that the oppressed group did not have. For example, they were permitted extra time at recess, were permitted to use the playground equipment and were able to receive second helpings at lunchtime. As a result, the oppressors believed that they were better than the group on the bottom and had the right to discriminate and engage in oppressive behavior. When the tables were turned the following day, instead of having empathy, the previously oppressed couldn't wait to have their turn on top so that they could discriminate against those who had oppressed them the day before.

Discrimination and Oppression are
Pervasive In Many Societies

Kim had been under the naïve impression that oppression was predominantly an American phenomenon until 2001, when she traveled "down under." There were oppressed groups in all three countries they visited:

- In Australia, the Europeans enjoyed positions of power while the Aborigines were oppressed.

- In New Zealand, again the Europeans enjoyed privilege while the Maori people were oppressed.

- In Fiji, the Eastern Indians were in power, while the native Fijians were oppressed.

One does not have to look far for present day examples of oppression. We need only look in the headlines of our newspapers. Today, African immigrants in France, who have been oppressed, were responding with riots in the streets. Consider what happened in Rwanda between the Hutus and Tutsis, who fought a civil war where the balance of power kept reversing. Whichever group was in power at a particular time oppressed the other group. Finally in 1994, the oppressed assumed the role of the brutal oppressors resulting in mass genocide.

It seems that the adage, "power corrupts" is true in many cases. When people get into positions of power and forget about working toward the common good, many abuses of power can occur, resulting in discrimination and oppression.

Cycle of Prejudice and Oppression

Bailey Jackson and Rita Hardiman first developed a model of the cycle of prejudice and oppression, which was modified by Joan Olsson in 1988.[2] The cycle begins when people engage in their natural tendency to group together based on similarities. When this occurs, similar people often close ranks when confronted by someone who looks or acts differently than they do. This reaction is generally based upon fear or a general sense of discomfort.

Unless someone from the group ventures out to learn something personal about the outsider, myths will most likely begin to be shared. People will make things up about the outsider to categorize him or her somehow. This misinformation will result in stereotyping. These stereotypes will then be reinforced by everything that makes up the culture: institutions such as government, schools, and churches; the media; and one's family and peers.

Eventually internalization occurs. The myths are believed to be truths and any differences from the group in power are recognized as deficits. During this internalization process, even the members of the oppressed group begin to believe the myths. This results in the oppressed experiencing lower self-esteem, self-doubt, and little hope for a better future.

Finally, the behaviors are played out as the people of the majority culture begin to act in prejudiced and oppressive ways. These behaviors then create, reinforce, and perpetuate the myths that began the cycle—and so the cycle becomes self-perpetuating.

The good news is that since these behaviors are all learned, they can be unlearned. To interrupt the cycle of prejudice and oppression, people must unlearn the myths and then relearn information about the target group based on personal interaction.

This unlearning and relearning process was clearly depicted in the movie, *American History X*. During this movie, a white supremacist went to prison for murdering a black man in cold blood. In prison, he found himself surrounded by the very people he hated. Based on a positive, personal relationship that the lead character formed with a black man in prison, he was able to unlearn the prejudices he had held his whole life. As a result he began to think differently about an entire race of people.

Many believe that discrimination and oppression ended in the 1960s. While it's true that the Civil Rights Act was passed in 1964 and the Equal Rights Amendment for women was passed in 1972, laws cannot legislate the non-public behavior of a country's citizenry.

Discrimination and Oppression Today

As a member of the majority culture, Kim was completely unaware of the different way she was treated compared to the way Sylvester was treated. Some of Kim's experiences as a white woman with Sylvester, a black man, in social settings were appalling. Even though they were not a couple but simply friends, most people perceived them to be one. Kim remembers one incident at a restaurant with Sylvester, when they did not receive service for 30 minutes, despite the fact that it was not a busy time and there were plenty of staff available to wait on them.

On more than one occasion, when they would enter a store together, they would go in separate directions. The sales person would follow Sylvester, asking to be of assistance but actually keeping a close eye on him for fear he may steal something. In the meantime, Kim would be left to roam around the store without any scrutiny. This is not unusual. A Caucasian woman admitted in diversity training that when she was younger, she and her friends had a shoplifting racquet going. She would enter a store with some black girlfriends; while the store clerks followed her friends around the store, she was able to steal things undetected.

When Kim and Sylvester began teaching diversity training in Pennsylvania, many participants in their trainings refused to believe that discrimination and oppression still exist in the United States today. They would concede that it was possible that they existed in some isolated instances in rural areas, but not in cities. What they refused to believe is that there are areas in the United States where a black person driving a nice car will get pulled over by the police, simply because of his skin color and his not belonging in that particular neighborhood. African-Americans call this a DWB—driving while black.

Many people of color will tell you that discrimination and oppression today are even more dangerous than they were years ago. At least in the past, discrimination and oppression were overt; a person knew where it was coming from. Blacks knew that they couldn't eat in a particular restaurant. They knew that they were not allowed to attend a certain school. They knew where they had to sit on the bus and where to use public restrooms. Although these were difficult realities, the consistency and obviousness helped those oppressed and discriminated against to make valuable decisions. However, today most racists are much more covert in their acts of discrimination.

This covert discrimination was made clear to Sylvester in high school by a white boy whom he considered to be a good friend. They were on the track team together. One day at the end of the track season, Sylvester was seated outside of school waiting for a ride home, when a pickup truck full of white males approached him. When they began to shout obscenities at him, Sylvester quickly leapt up and ran for the door to get back in school. As he banged on the door, he saw his friend looking at him. Sylvester felt a great deal of relief until he saw his friend turn and walk away. Sylvester's relief turned into panic. He ran two blocks to a store where he called a family member to come and pick him up. When he got the opportunity to talk with his "friend," he was quickly made aware of the fact that they really were not friends. Sylvester had been a track star and was special to the team, but now that track was over, this other boy didn't need to be nice to Sylvester. Even though this angered Sylvester it offered him a useful lesson in prejudice.

Prejudice can be Unlearned

Much research has been done in the area of prejudice. Since prejudice is learned, it can be unlearned. The unlearning process requires mostly a willingness to unlearn, and experiences with and empathy for the oppressed individuals. Research shows that people with high self-esteem and high self-acceptance tend to have a low degree of prejudice.[3] It seems that when people know who they are and like themselves, there is no reason to discriminate against others.

Interestingly, research shows that social class prejudice may be stronger in the United States than either racial or religious prejudice.[4]

However, it is very difficult to separate the individual factors of race and socioeconomic status. Most poor people in this country are people of color. People of color who are not poor have achieved a certain degree of assimilation which makes them more acceptable to the majority culture.

Research also indicates that facts alone are not sufficient to reduce prejudice.[5] Rather, a climate that fosters open discussion of negative feelings is needed, to encourage a shift to more positive attitudes. Gaining an understanding of the cycle of stereotyping and prejudice is also helpful, as is social contact between the different groups. The amount of time spent learning about a group is directly related to the reduction in prejudice.

Research shows that media can be used effectively to improve attitudes between groups.[6] This is no surprise since movies and other media have played an important part in reinforcing stereotypes. Often, when we read articles, stories, or books, our minds will drift visualizing the race and gender of the person described in our reading. The words we read produce a mental image based on preconceived ideas about the character. If we read a headline that states, "Two teenage students enter school and go on a shooting rampage" we form a visual of these students based on stereotypes. Some movies that we have found helpful for challenging these stereotypes are *American History X, Higher Learning, Men of Honor,* and *Ghosts of Mississippi.*

Cultural Sensitivity is the First Step

The purpose of this book, up to this point, has been to help management and employees develop a sense of cultural sensitivity. Cultural sensitivity is the ability to empathize and to relate to some of the challenges and pleasures a person from a different cultural group might experience. Cultural sensitivity enables a person from the majority culture to be a little more understanding of members from minority groups. It also assists minority groups to better understand the psychology and motivation of the majority culture. This mutual understanding is an essential key to the success of a diversity program in the workplace.

Many companies have a reactive approach when dealing with cultural issues. A new person is hired. She is a woman, while most of the employees in this company are men. Before hiring the woman, the supervisor asks her if she would have any difficulty working with men. Eager to get the job she responds, "Not at all." Oftentimes management will ask the right questions in evaluating potential employees, to determine if they will fit with the team already in place. However, management sometimes will fail to prepare the team for the new member.

After the woman has been working for a few weeks in the organization, everyone is beginning to feel comfortable. This comfort is most often the catalyst to many acts of discrimination or oppression. The feelings that we carry inside of us oftentimes are displayed when our comfort level is increased or when we are feeling very confident. As the weeks go by, the men begin to get "friendly" with the woman. They share stories, anecdotes, and jokes while on lunch break. Everyone seems to be getting along well—joking, laughing, and having a good time. However, many of these stories are tainted with stereotypes: judging liberals, judging homosexuals, judging a particular ethnic group or religious sect. These stories create a strong degree of discomfort in the woman because, unbeknownst to the men, she belongs to all of these groups.

After weeks of enduring these judgments, she decides to go to her supervisor. She tells him of her dilemma, which he promises to address. He sends out a memo and calls a special meeting. However, a simple edict from on high does not motivate employees to seek to understand other workers who may be different from them. The men begin to suspect that someone has complained about them, and they don't like it. They figure that it must be the woman, since none of this happened before she came along.

In their anger, they begin to set limits regarding what they will say in her presence. They don't have lunch with her anymore. They begin to whisper and make comments that she overhears and doesn't like. After several months of this treatment, she decides to go to the union and file a grievance. Once the grievance is filed and substantiated, management makes it mandatory for all employees to attend training sessions on Diversity. This is like installing smoke detectors AFTER the fire has started.

Discrimination and Oppression at Work

Discrimination can eat at the very core of any company's existence. When people are not working together in a spirit of harmony, a company's bottom line will suffer. Oftentimes the only employees who feel the pinch of discrimination are those who are being discriminated against. Discrimination feels comfortable for the oppressor. When you are sharing a blanket with someone, and he or she pulls the covering and takes most of it from you, that person feels comfortable even though you don't. It is the same with oppression.

The best way to defeat acts of discrimination and oppression is to be proactive. Know that we all have biases which, if not managed effectively, can lead to suspensions, firings, grievances, lawsuits and settlements.

Imagine that you are a supervisor and Archie Bunker works for you. Archie is a hard worker; he comes to work on time everyday and doesn't mind working overtime. He is totally committed to the company. However, Archie has no problem sharing his prejudiced views. He doesn't even understand that they are discriminatory; he just knows that they feel right to him. Many of the people who work with Archie share the same views and don't mind Archie's comments. But there are some who really don't appreciate his comments. After receiving several complaints, how do you effectively manage this situation? Archie has been touted for his work ethic and his commitment to the company, so he doesn't see this coming. How will he feel about being disciplined for his comments?

We have heard many people say, "We don't have to like each other to work together." This is true. You don't have to like everyone, nor do you have to agree with their point of view. However it is important that you understand and respect each other. A lack of understanding and respect can easily lead to alienation or discrimination. In sports, athletes and coaches have disagreements all the time. Two players for the Philadelphia Eagles were having some difficulties which ultimately ended in suspension. Discrimination and oppression will do absolutely nothing to enhance one's work environment. When these elements are at work, people suffer. Relationships are lost and the bottom line, your profit, is affected.

Children use discrimination techniques at a very early age; as adults we can learn from this. Whenever children become angry with each other, one child (usually the one with the perceived power) will say, "I'm not your friend anymore." This is similar to the treatment the newly hired woman received on her new job—and the treatment that many women and people of color receive. The words "I'm not your friend anymore" represent our desire to separate ourselves from those who are different from us or who don't agree with our position. Taking away our friendship is an act of discrimination.

Many companies don't fully grasp the importance of having the team understand the significance of cultural sensitivity. For many companies, the reality of discrimination and oppression doesn't sink in until an event occurs . . . a friendship is dissolved. This problem can be managed and avoided, but managers must believe that it is an issue—even if it is invisible. They must know that it is there before they see it. Managing discrimination in the workplace is like magic, NOW YOU SEE IT, NOW YOU DON'T!

In the next chapter we will discuss Majority Privilege—the privileges enjoyed by the majority culture which are not available to other members of that society.

Majority Privilege

Majority privilege is enjoyed by the majority culture—without them even being aware of it. Kim grew up in a small, country town where the greatest diversity factor was religious in nature. The citizens in her town were divided among those who attended the Catholic Church, those who attended one of the two other Protestant churches, and those who did not attend church. Catholics didn't date Protestants and Protestants didn't date Catholics. (As for those who didn't attend church, they were pretty much free to date whomever they liked.) The point is that there were no people of color in this town whatsoever.

Kim had no exposure to anyone who lacked the privileges that she enjoyed. As a young child, when Kim wanted a doll, her mother had no trouble finding a doll that looked like her—that she could relate to. When she bought greeting cards for her friends, there was no lack of cards with Caucasian faces. She had no problem finding people to date who had a similar background to hers.

At one point during her high school years, a black teenager began attending her school; he was living in a foster home. Only in retrospect, does Kim wonder what that experience was like for him. There were no people who looked like him. There were no products in stores representing his culture. He might have felt as if he had been sent to Mars.

Majority Privilege Still Exists Today

Most members of the white majority in the United States want to believe that the civil rights movement of the 1960s eradicated racism in this country. It offends the sensibilities to believe that in 2006, blacks could *still* be treated differently than whites. However, you have only to ask a person of color in the United States if they have the same privileges that whites do, to learn that racism still exists.

Kim has heard numerous stories from friends who say it's very common for a black male to be pulled over by a police officer for driving in a particular neighborhood, especially at night. Recently Kim saw two different pictures of survivors of Hurricane Katrina on the Internet. One picture showed two white people; the other a black man. The caption under the white survivors read, "Survivors found food from grocer's store." The caption under the black survivor read, "Gets food after looting store."

The subject of majority privilege is a difficult one. Some people of color are offended to be reminded that white people in the United States enjoy privileges simply because of the color of their skin. However, most people of color are relieved when they hear a white person acknowledging this imbalance in our system. After all, people of color live with the obvious existence of this imbalance everyday, but most members of the majority culture don't even seem to notice. We don't notice because our privilege is an unconscious part of our day-to-day existence. It's something that just *is*, like the air we breathe. It's an inherent part of our culture.

As young people are developing their racial identity, they look for role models in people who are similar to them. White youths generally see that people who look like them are running things. White people are in positions of power throughout this country. However young people of color see very few examples of people who look like they do in positions of power. The few people of color who have achieved positions of power are broadly recognized for learning to "act white," which unfortunately is usually necessary to achieve advancement and financial success. It's quite rare to find a person of color in a position of power who is maintaining a strong racial or ethnic identity.

What this demonstrates is that in order to get ahead at work, women and people of color must give up their cultural identity, at least in the workplace. This is a supreme example of white privilege. Can you even imagine, as a white person, being told that in order to get a promotion you have to act like a person of color? My guess is that you would be outraged!

People in Power Don't Even Recognize They Have Privilege

The insidious thing about white, majority privilege is that those who have it really aren't aware of it. Caucasian children in the United States see people just like them in power; things are as they should be. Life is just and fair. There are no social ills to fight against. Caucasians grow up believing that since things are fair for them, they must be fair for everyone else.

Many Caucasians don't want to accept that they enjoy privileges that people of color don't. In fact, with the unfortunate use of a well-intentioned quota system, many Caucasians still complain about the unfair advantage people of color have in certain fields where the quota system is still employed. They complain about reverse discrimination, which we will discuss in Chapter 13.

While it is undeniable that there have been instances when more qualified white people did not get the job because people of color were hired, these situations occurred only to individuals—not to an entire race of people, as has been the history of African-Americans in the United States. If a white person doesn't get a job on the police force, he can get a job as a probation officer. However, a person of color experiencing difficulty being hired will continue to have difficulty wherever he goes.

This majority privilege permeates all of society. In school systems, many standardized tests have been shown to be culturally biased.

What this means is that the tests are assessing knowledge that is not necessarily common to cultures other than the white, middle-class, dominant culture. If white students were given a test on Ebonics, they probably wouldn't do very well either!

More on the Blue Eyes, Brown Eyes Exercise

Many white people have taken offence at the mention of majority privilege. When it is brought to their attention, they may resent even the suggestion that they have a privilege. This was very clearly demonstrated when Jane Elliott conducted her famous blue eyes/brown eyes exercise with Oprah's audience.

Most white members of the audience were appalled that Ms. Elliott would even suggest that they were racist. They were not able to look at the possibility that racism and white privilege are woven into the very fabric of the United States. They certainly weren't able to admit that by virtue of their own skin color, they were a member of the racist system.

Another point of privilege illuminated by Ms. Elliott's exercise is that oppressed people don't enjoy the same ability to excel in the academic arena. During her exercise, Ms. Elliot administered tests to her students in the form of card packs. Without fail, the group of students wearing the collars identifying them as inferior, performed much worse during the card pack testing. On the other hand, those without the collars performed better than they had previously. When asked what made the difference, the children wearing the collars were quick to point out they had difficulty thinking of anything other than the collars, which took away the privilege they were used to enjoying.

Heterosexual Privilege

One of the least talked about privileges is heterosexual privilege. Heterosexuals share a privilege in the workplace that affects those who are not heterosexual.

In many businesses, employees try to make their surroundings comfortable. They may decorate their lockers or put pictures up in their offices. When you walk into someone's office, the inhabitant will often have pictures of his or her family on the desk. The children or significant others visiting feel good when they see their picture; they feel loved, appreciated, and honored.

Now consider employees who are not heterosexual. They too have special people in their lives—people whom they care about and would love to put on display. However, they need to consider their co-workers' values and belief systems. Will their partner's picture be accepted by others? What will be the implications of displaying their pictures? Will it be safe to do so?

Furthermore, when the holiday parties come around, homosexuals will consider the level of acceptance of the group before they decide to invite their partner. Let's consider the often taboo subject of public displays of affection. Whether or not you engage in them yourself, many people do. When a husband's wife drops by to see him at work, he will often rise from his desk and give her a hug and a kiss. Can you imagine the anxiety that a homosexual experiences at the mere thought of hugging and kissing his or her partner in public?

Regardless of whether you approve of homosexuality, our point is simply that heterosexuals enjoy privileges that homosexuals don't.

Privilege at Work
White privilege, physically-abled privilege, and economic privilege, are just some of the privileges that can perpetuate separation amongst individuals—and certainly amongst co-workers.

Oftentimes, the privileged group, in order to feel more comfortable, will expect the "inferior" group to change its behavior. It doesn't occur to the privileged group to become more appreciative or accepting.

Imagine that you work in a company of about 300 people. As far as you know, everyone in the company is pretty much just like you. You share the same sexual orientation, the same ethnicity, and similar economic status. One day a man is hired who is somewhat different. Although he has the same sexual orientation and similar economic status, he is of a different ethnic group. You like him, but you don't realize that because of his ethnicity he experiences different treatment than you when he is out in public. Although you really enjoy spending time with him, he is extremely uncomfortable in certain environments that you enjoy.

You go out to lunch with a group of colleagues and are having a good time when you notice that your new co-worker seems somewhat distant. You ask him what is wrong and he says nothing. (It can be difficult to verbalize feelings of discomfort when you are not a part of the privileged culture.) As time passes, your new co-worker stops going out with you and your colleagues. He begins spending more time alone and less time with you. You approach him again and an argument ensues.

You just don't understand what the problem is. You know that you have been respectful and supportive of him, and yet he continues to distance himself from you. Your relationship soon dissolves. You and your co-worker have created an environment that is uncomfortable for everyone involved. Who is at fault? Although neither party has done anything to purposefully cause this separation, the relationship failed because there was no understanding or discussion around privilege.

Privilege Must be Recognized and Discussed

Because privilege is generally not discussed in the workplace, most managers believe that they have no diversity problems at work. Whenever management looks out at its workforce, all the employees seem to be doing their jobs. Members of the privileged group often think that everything is fine. When members of a non-privileged group are asked how things are going, they may also say everything is fine—but it's possibly because they fear that being honest may jeopardize their job. Even though honest discussions of issues in the workplace will undoubtedly be uncomfortable, have them anyway and commit to work through the difficult times.

It is important that companies all over the world hold discussions around issues of culture and diversity. Developing an understanding of others is critical to camaraderie in the workplace. We should not assume that everyone enjoys the same privileges as we do, because they don't. As we move toward a more cohesive work environment, we must develop a sense of compassion for those who are different.

Sylvester works as a program director with young children in a low-income area of Chicago. Many of these children are black, from single parent homes. Sylvester spoke with several people in the school system to see if they had any suggestions to improve these kids' academic and social experiences. Although people came up with suggestions that were very positive, they were not sensitive to the group. Implementing their ideas would require facilitation from a member of the privileged culture, because in this case non-privileged people are not heard when they go into a school board meeting. Non-privileged people are not respected when they approach a school official and ask questions. Non-privileged people are not acknowledged when they make phone calls to school officials. It's sad but true. The fact that school officials did not recognize this was disturbing..

Sylvester didn't discount the suggestions he heard. He realized that many suggestions were good, even though they required a person with privilege to implement them. Sylvester began to meet with individuals whom he thought could help in his mission. This process was difficult; oftentimes the non-privileged will resist assistance from the privileged because of a lack of trust and understanding. This lack of trust exists because the non-privileged group clearly sees the freedoms of the privileged group, which the privileged group is not acknowledging.

Therefore, trust needed to be developed between the privileged and the non-privileged groups, so that they could work together.

This required members of the privileged group to disclose and share their thoughts and feelings, which is not always easy. Oftentimes members of the privileged group feel that they have to apologize for the freedoms they enjoy—which is not the case. However, if privileged groups have perpetrated injustices against other groups to obtain these freedoms, then they should apologize for the injustice. Bringing these two groups together—the privileged and the not—can be difficult. In this case, Sylvester shifted the focus to the children, which helped. Once the groups were able to look at the problem at hand, things started to come together.

Leveling the Playing Field

Understanding majority privilege can be difficult for some. The word privilege means to have an advantage—a right or certain freedoms that others don't enjoy. Many of us want to feel that society is moving in the direction of equity, but the fact is that some continue to enjoy privileges that others don't. When you are identified as being part of the group that enjoys privilege, you may become defensive or feel that it is just not true. Well, it *is* true. The good news is that there is something that you as an individual can do to level the playing field.

First of all, recognize that you do have privilege. Denying it doesn't change the reality. Having privilege does not make you a bad person. It just is! When you recognize that you are privileged, you can begin to separate yourself from the pack and make a difference.

Next, you can begin to acknowledge that members of the non-privileged groups are not wrong, they are not bad, they are just different. When the judgments are removed, we can look at other groups more objectively and appreciate their differences. Understand that when people from a different group than yours are in your presence, they may be having an experience that is different than yours. Your objectivity will help them understand that they don't have to experience their experience the way they are experiencing it! You can become a voice of support and understanding. You can become a catalyst for change.

Lastly, encourage non-privileged people through genuine acceptance. It is important that they aren't made to feel out of place or wrong. One of the things that we do, when we go around the country to provide diversity workshops, is to encourage youth workers to make their offices a safe place for homosexuals. Many teenagers who are not "out" have a difficult time finding people whom they can trust, to discuss their sexuality. There are steps that can be taken to let them know that you are a safe person to talk to.

We are not sure that there will come a day where there is no longer a group with privilege. There will probably always be people who have freedoms that others do not. What we would like to see, however, is a society where everyone understands and accepts the concept of privilege, and is more understanding and appreciative of non-privileged people.

In the next chapter, we will discuss the development of racial identity and how majority privilege impacts it.

Identity Development

As stated in Chapter 5, when children are newborns, they are fairly egocentric, focusing solely on meeting their own needs. As infants grow older, their world expands from themselves to include their immediate family members, particularly their primary caregiver. As time goes on, additional family members and other familiar people are added to the child's circle of influence. Over time, children's boundaries expand beyond their families to their friends and immediate community.

Even as adults, people feel safest and most comfortable with people who are familiar and who resemble them. Their comfort zone typically does not stretch beyond what is familiar; when they leave the realm of the familiar, their comfort level declines.

Let's compare the differences between the identity development of a child born into a family of the powerful dominant culture with that of a child born into a family from the minority culture.

Dominant Group Identity Development

The experience of children from the dominant culture, on an unconscious level, is that those who look like them are in power. Their people are the decision-makers, control the wealth, and have privileges that others don't. Children deduct that they are entitled to the same rights and privileges, since those in power are like them in terms of race, gender, and religion. They also assume that they will achieve the same accomplishments as the adults in their group. As a result, children born into the dominant culture develop positive self-esteem, confidence, self-worth, socially acceptable goals and desires, and a sense of entitlement.

In the United States, the group in power is still predominantly Caucasian men of European dissent. However, as Dr. Ruby Payne addresses in her book, *A Framework for Understanding Poverty*, the dominant group is based more on socioeconomic status and the ability to access resources that are not readily available to others. The dominant group has the money it needs to purchase goods and services. It also has the ability to "choose and control emotional responses, particularly to negative situations, without engaging in self-destructive behavior. This is an internal resource and shows itself through stamina, perseverance, and choices. The dominant group has the necessary mental abilities and skills to manage daily living, such as reading, writing and computation."

Members of the dominant group generally have spiritual beliefs that recognize "divine purpose and guidance." They tend to have physical health and mobility. They enjoy a strong support network of friends, family, and "backup resources . . . to access in times of need. These are external resources." The group in power has "frequent access to adult(s) who are appropriate, who are *nurturing* to the child and who do not engage in self-destructive behavior." They also understand the unspoken habits and rules of their group.[1]

It doesn't matter much whether we consider the dominant group in the United States to be those with socioeconomic status or Caucasians, as these groups are practically identical. The 2003 US Bureau of the Census statistics showed that 14.3% of White children live in poverty, while 29.7% of Hispanics, 31.9% of Native American, and 34.1% of African-American children live in poverty. This demonstrates Caucasians have more resources available to them, while people of color have limited financial and social resources.[2]

Minority Group Identity Development

Contrast the identity development of the dominant group with that of the non-dominant group. Children from minority groups notice that most adults who are like them are not in positions of power and do not enjoy privilege. They grow up knowing that they are the same as these adults and therefore have the same limited rights. Many fall into the cycle of becoming what they see around them. The discriminating treatment they receive becomes acceptable and a natural way of life for many of them. This mentality leads to a very negative and dismal outlook. They come to believe that the members of their minority group, including themselves, are not as good as those who are in power.

Of course, there are instances of people of color becoming prominent in areas such as sports or the entertainment world, which is why many young people of color aspire to be athletes, actors, and vocalists. While there may also be people of color who are in positions of power in corporate America, these people have often taken on the attitudes and characteristics of the majority culture. Young people of color have difficulty emulating them because they present such a discrepant image from the youngsters' daily experience.

Not only do young minorities notice that, for the most part, those who look and act like them do not enjoy privilege, but they often observe situations where the adult members of their group experience prejudice, discrimination, and oppression. Minority children are exposed to stereotypes about themselves and others like them, on a daily basis. They come to believe these negative stereotypes and, as a result, develop low self-esteem, a lack of confidence, and feelings of low self-worth.

Add to this the fact that minorities do not enjoy many of the resources available to the dominant group, as Dr. Payne writes. They don't always have the means to purchase goods and services they need. They are not always "in control of their emotional responses, particularly in negative situations" and "often engage in self-destructive behavior." Because of limited resources, many are unable to read, write and compute well enough to deal with daily life. There may be a lack of "belief in divine purpose" of today, while waiting for a better life in the hereafter. Those of lower economic status don't have the resources necessary to ensure good "physical health and mobility." They often don't have friends and family who are able to support them in times of need. The relationships and role models available to them often "engage in self-destructive behavior."[3]

For years minority groups and others have worked diligently to overcome prejudice, discrimination, and oppression. Affirmative Action was started in an effort to provide minorities and women with more opportunities for employment and education. Civil Rights legislation was passed in an effort to eliminate the unfair treatment of minority groups. Despite these commendable efforts to provide equality, we still have a society which is divided between those with privilege and those without. The fact remains that we still have a lot of work to do before we can truly say that all people are living in harmony and equality.

A Conversation about Power Difference

An African-American friend recently visited Kim. This man engaged Kim's son, Dave, in several intellectual conversations regarding race. He spoke to Dave about black people in his neighborhood who look to the media for signs of success and then attempt to emulate what they see. Dave countered with, "Bill Gates is a real successful white man but I don't try to look like him." The man responded, "Of course you don't. You are surrounded by successful people in your family who look just like you do. You don't have to get your role models from the media."

He then went on to point out that Dave's family gatherings usually include a man who owns a lumber company, a man who has his own engineering business, a man who owns a sign business, a man who has an excavating business—not to mention Dave's mother who has her own training, coaching, and consulting business. When Dave's father was alive, he had his own successful automotive repair business. Therefore, it would be logical for Dave to grow up believing that he too can achieve this measure of success. In fact, he should strive for that and more, to live up to family expectations.

The African-American man went on to explain that black children growing up in his neighborhood don't have these types of people at their family gatherings. They often don't even know who their fathers are, or if they do know, they have no relationships with them. Many black children know people who have been shot, are alcoholics or drug addicts, are on welfare, and barely make ends meet. Since there is little success in their immediate surroundings they are seeking success in billboards, radio, television, and the movies. Minorities will often strive to achieve things that represent success—such as a nice car, fashionable clothes, jewelry, and a certain type of alcohol to drink. Unfortunately, these things just provide the illusion of success, and use up whatever limited resources are available to the minorities.

DiversityInc reports that "the racial diversity within Fortune 500 executive offices has been changing very slowly. And the proportion of people of color in leadership roles remains far beneath their ever-increasing representation in the population. For example, there were no black Fortune 500 CEOs in 1995. Blacks comprise 12.2 percent of the U.S. population . . . today, there only are six black CEOs of Fortune 500 companies. . . Latinos comprise 14.2 percent of the population. But . . . there are just four Latino CEOs at Fortune 500 companies . . . There are six Asian-American CEOs at Fortune 500 companies . . . Asian-Americans make up 4.2 percent of the population.

The political power base continues to be dominated by white men ...There is only one black senator . . . and 42 black representatives . . . There are three Latino senators . . . There are 27 Latino Congressional representatives . . . There are two Asian-American senators . . . [and] . . . just five Asian-Americans serve in the House."[4]

There is clearly an unequal distribution of power in the United States resulting in majority privilege.

The "Race Card"

Kim was recently speaking to two Caucasian women, Kathy and Teresa, about this book, *Leveraging Diversity at Work*. Both were interested in its subject matter and had strong opinions about it. Kathy had come from virtually nothing, being a shampoo girl, to owning her own hair salon—through sheer determination, sacrifice, and hard work. Teresa had been in the corporate arena, the only woman working in a man's world.

Teresa completely understood how difficult it is for a woman to compete in a man's world. In order to get ahead, Teresa often had to place her career before family matters, which caused her great intrapersonal conflict. Unlike women, however, she felt that blacks are always playing the "race card." She believes that blacks use their minority status as a reason for unfair treatment, when perhaps it has nothing to do with race. Kathy also echoed this belief, and questioned why blacks can't simply work hard to get out of poverty and debt. Why can't they simply recognize what needs to be done and do whatever it takes, as she had done?

What these two women hadn't considered was the role that early childhood messages play in a person's identity development, which we spoke of in Chapters 4 and 5. Children who are raised within a group that perceives itself as powerless receive vastly different messages than those raised in the majority culture. Minorities do not receive the messages "You can be anything you put your mind to being." "You can make anything happen if you work hard enough." or "Starting your own business is a great idea." These messages are generally messages of the majority culture.

Research is starting to prove that our thoughts determine our reality. If we think we can, then we do. If we are convinced of our failure, then we are defeated before we even begin. Research further demonstrates that if we were able to take the wealth that exists in the entire world and distribute it evenly among all people, in a very short time the majority of the wealth would be back in the hands of the wealthy and the poor would stay poor. Why? Because our minds are programmed early on with messages of what we deserve and what is likely for us. These messages are firmly implanted in our brains, and our brains create our reality to match what is already believed internally. [5]

This is why it is important for adults to encourage young people to move upward in society. This can be difficult when the adults feel defeated themselves. Our environment is very critical to our identity development. While a minority child from the inner city can grow up to achieve great things, the odds are currently against it.

The Identity Journey

Identity is important to all of us. It tells us who we are and who we want to become. It acts as a blueprint for us in designing our destiny. Many individuals whom we encounter as adults are continuing their identity journey. Some have not yet completed their identity development, and may therefore be shifting and showing uncertainty in their movement.

A developed identity means the difference between having a job and having a career. Career-minded individuals have a better grasp of their identity; they have decided on an occupation which will enhance or compliment who they are. Many minorities, on the other hand, are focused on having a job just to pay the bills—either because their identity is that of a survivor or because they are still continuing along the identity development journey.

A person's position on this identity journey plays a big part in his or her management style. In many families, children will identify one parent as the disciplinarian and the other as the more permissive parent. Depending on the situation, children will gravitate towards the parent who will be the most beneficial to them. In companies, when managers are wavering and uncertain about their own identity, they may not be consistent in their directives; this can be a problem for many of the employees, and for the company.

Since people are going to be at different points in their identity development, there will be varying degrees of commitment to the company. Some employees will identify their jobs as careers. They will bring a great deal of creativity and initiative to the job. They will be willing to go above and beyond the call of duty, working with a high level of energy. The work that they do will be fulfilling and will support who they are—their identity. These people usually have a great deal of ambition. They believe in the work they are doing and enjoy it.

On the other hand, other employees will identify their position as a job. These employees will probably come to work regularly, will be punctual, will not cause many problems, and will perform adequately. However, they will not take much initiative and won't bring any innovation to their work. If they have developed an identity that "you work to live," then that's just what they will do. They may not enjoy their work, but they are satisfied with simply having a job.

Recognizing the differences in employees' progress toward their own identity development is important; identities that are not clearly defined could create problems. A manager should help nurture employees who are continuing along their journey.

Nurturing the Development

Being in an environment where your role is not defined can be scary. Imagine being a member of a team and not knowing exactly where you fit in. You understand the concept and the plan, but you just are not sure what your specific role is. You struggle through meetings; the day-to-day grind becomes more than you can handle. You are not sure what to do, but you know that you don't want to lose your position.

Eventually you become frustrated and it starts showing in your work. You no longer give your all and you begin to project a very lackadaisical manner. Your effort and participation is viewed by others as negative and begins to affect the overall camaraderie within the company. As management begins to evaluate the situation, you may be viewed as the problem because you are not a team player. However you just are working within your poorly defined identity as a team member.

Understanding that some employees may be working to identify themselves will give managers the opportunity to nurture their development. Employees who have a continuing education process incorporated into their jobs are employees who are more likely to move in a direction with which they can comfortably identify.

When employees are encouraged to explore their likes and dislikes, they can better understand their direction, which in turn makes them more effective employees. They may not remain in their present position as they develop an understanding of what position is more appropriate for them. This is a risk that many managers don't want to take. But the fact is, it's better to have employees who clearly understand their identity and work within it rather than to have hard-working employees who don't identify with what they do.

The next chapter will present Mr. Marcus C. Gentry's opinions about the supreme importance of valuing oneself as a unique creation with unique talents, skills and abilities. This is particularly critical for women and minorities.

Valuing Oneself

by Marcus C. Gentry a.k.a. "Dr. R.E.S.P.E.C.T."

In order to value yourself, you must first become aware of who you are—which means knowing your strengths and weaknesses—physically, emotionally, mentally, and spiritually. Imagine, if you will, being given a box and told to keep that box for 10, 20, 50 or more years to do whatever you want with it. How much value would you place on that box without knowing the contents? You would most likely look at other people with boxes to see what they were doing with theirs, model their box-handling behavior, and view their box limitations and successes as your own—not realizing that your box contains unique treasures, gems, jewels, and tools. In fact, your box is different than any other box, just as your life is which you were gifted at birth.

The Miracle of Birth: A Success Story

To truly value the person we are today, we must go back to our beginning. Between 200 and 600 million sperm cells travel on a heat censored course towards the upper end of the fallopian tubes where conception usually occurs. Only about 100 reach that area. The reproductive tract that is traveled by the cells is considered to be a very hostile environment—course and dangerous even to healthy cells. (Twenty percent of the cells are likely to be defective.) This reproductive tract is acidic, containing antibodies that seek out and destroy sperm cells, absorbing the rest into the body system. Only one sperm cell survives the course.[1]

This one sperm has the endurance, the determination, the focus of direction, the speed, and the strength to reach and penetrate the ovum, which then develops into a single embryo that will become a fetus. The development during the next 38 weeks or so leads to the birth of a child. Our very existence on our day of birth is the story of a TRUE survivor—one who has already experienced beating the odds, overcoming obstacles, and functioning well under pressure. With such a great victory under our belt how do we lose our personal value?

Beware the Enemy

As children, we used our creativity to experience our new environment. We recognized our need to touch, taste, travel, and see all that was available to us. If we saw something that was not available to us at that time, we improvised, adapted, and overcame without hesitation.

However, our parents or guardians, in their desire to keep us safe, began to put restrictions on us based on their experience and conditioned beliefs. We began to do the things that would bring rewards and diminish painful consequences. In many ways we developed a sense of good and bad, right and wrong, based on reward or punishment from our caretakers.

When we mature in a healthy environment, we develop a personal sense of values. However, everyone does not always exist and operate in a safe, healthy, and fair environment. There are individuals who gain power, wealth, and worth, on the backs of others. Many who are not careful become overly dependent on the opinions and standards of others, which are not always in their best interest. Therefore, they become bricks in someone else's dream, instead of being the architects of their own destiny.

As Carter G. Woodson stated, "If you can control a man's thinking, you don't have to worry about his actions. If you can determine what a man thinks you do not have to worry about what he will do. If you can make a man believe that he is inferior, you don't have to compel him to seek an inferior status, he will do so without being told and if you can make a man believe that he is justly an outcast, you don't have to order him to the back door, he will go to the back door on his own and if there is no back door, the very nature of the man will demand that you build one."[2]

Thus, many people who were born true champions, against all odds, have allowed the enemy on the outside to become the enemy within. When such individuals, who have lost their sense of personal value, are placed in another hostile environment similar to the reproductive tract, instead of becoming strong survivors again, they fall into the rule of "Association bringing Assimilation." They either become chameleon-like characters or they blend into the dominant culture without a real sense of what they have to offer. This behavior is then rewarded or has negative consequences.

The rewards may look like acceptance in the family, job promotion, or admission into certain clubs or organizations. But the negative consequences should not be minimized: being labeled as arrogant as opposed to confident and ostracized from their peers. The psychological damage that can result from this ostracism causes many to not seek their own personal value, unless it matches the values of the dominant culture. Many would rather be discontented than different.

Overcoming the Enemy
The enemy is any person or any system that perpetuates ideas, behaviors, or language that demeans, demoralizes, or disrespects the personal worth of an individual. *The Art of War* teaches that success in battle depends on the knowledge of oneself and knowledge of the enemy.[3] In assessing the knowledge of our self we must honestly ask ourselves if we have a sincere desire to recognize our value and carry ourselves in harmony with that knowledge. Are we willing to put in the required work?

People who are not willing or able to identify their own personal values, and exist in an environment where individual expression is not encouraged, often acculturate, blending in with the dominant culture. Acculturation brings benefits such as reduced conflict with the dominant culture and rewards such as invitations to certain social functions.

Regaining Our Value

You start regaining your value by surrounding yourself with people who value, understand, and have respect for your cultural experience and your personal value. Next, you generate opportunities for your own creative expression. Then you place importance on spending time alone, and treating/valuing yourself as you would like others to treat/value you.

Achieving Value Above and Beyond

Oftentimes, when people develop a clear sense of identity, they search for arenas where their value can be appreciated. Basically, everyone wants to be recognized and applauded as valuable. However, when people are in situations where value is determined by criteria that they cannot achieve, an effective method—considered to be one of the *22 Immutable Laws of Marketing*[4]—is to establish an area that they can be "first" in, or an area of expertise within the constraints of their environment.

Marcus Garvey says, "Let us not waste time in breathless appeals to the strong while we are weak, but lend our time, energy and effort to the accumulation of strength among ourselves by which we will voluntarily attract the attention of others."[5] In our efforts to achieve value for ourselves above and beyond the average, it is important to remember some key points mentioned in *The Art of War*. We must turn our focus from knowledge of ourselves to knowledge of the enemy.[6]

Personal value in our culture is not determined by the extent of joy, peace, and love in our life, nor is it determined by a contented mind or the quality of our character. We currently live in a society where personal value is determined by the acquisition of material goods. Particularly in minority communities, the media presents an over-saturation of alcohol ads, showing people who appear to be living the "good life." This leads to people in these communities consuming alcohol under the illusion that they are gaining value by modeling what they see. Also promoted in these communities are possessions that depreciate with time instead of appreciating, resulting in people becoming greater consumers rather than producers. This not only gives people a false sense of value, camouflaging what real value is, but it oftentimes causes financial distress.

In order to recognize, maintain, and build our genuine value, we must take the time to identify and appreciate who we are, differentiating between true value and the debilitating illusion. We must also recognize the existence of a system that benefits from those who are uninformed and undereducated.

They say that a lion cub born in captivity can be raised successfully in that environment and become somewhat domesticated, performing tricks and providing entertainment for its master. However, if that cub is allowed in the jungle around non-domesticated lions, it will never return to that same state of domestication because it realizes its true value and identity. Value yourself.

Tips for the Employer

People are responsible for their own value or lack thereof. We are not suggesting that the role of the employer is to become a social worker or psychologist. However, there are strategies that can be implemented to create an environment conducive for people, who currently may not be operating from the highest awareness of their value, to thrive and grow in your business.

The following are excerpts of some of the principles that are taught to the men and women of R.E.S.P.E.C.T. who deliver empowerment trainings.[7] These principles also apply when providing an atmosphere in the workplace for employees to perform with a sense of value.

1. Employers must first value and respect themselves, maintaining a high sense of personal integrity and a strong business ethic.

2. Employers must know their own personal strengths and weaknesses, as well as those of their business, in order to effectively inspire others.

3. Employers must not be intimidated by their employees.

4. Employers must respect their employees.

5. Employers must provide a safe environment for open and honest communication.

6. Rapport must come before rules, regulations, and expectations, in order for employees to function at peak performance.

7. Employers must get to know their employees as individuals, to provide an environment that acknowledges the value of employees.

8. Employers must provide training programs that assist their employees to function well under pressure.

9. Employers must maintain the energy necessary to provide a value-enhancing environment for their employees, beyond special events.

10. Last by not least, employers must master communication between themselves and their employees, acknowledging the value of the employees' presence, ideas, and suggestions.

The next chapter will discuss the expansion of our consciousness that can occur when we leave our comfort zones with an open mind and a willing spirit.

Leaving Your Comfort Zone

"Knowledge is the antidote to fear."
—Ralph Waldo Emerson

How accepting we are of differences and the way we value diversity depend on the experiences we have had with people from different ethnic groups, socioeconomic classes, religions, age groups or communities. The first factor is whether or not we have had any experiences with a different culture; the second factor is whether these experiences were generally positive or negative. People who have had positive experiences with members of a different culture are often more objective and willing to value diversity.

Feelings of apprehension, loneliness, isolation, and lack of confidence are common when visiting another culture. If you have ever been the only person of a particular group, you probably have experienced some of these feelings. In different situations, Kim has been the only Caucasian, the only woman, the youngest, or the oldest. Similarly, Sylvester has experienced being the only African-American, the only male, the youngest, and the oldest. During each occurrence, they felt some discomfort and uncertainty about how they were being perceived and what behaviors were expected of them. Have you ever been the only person of a particular group? What feelings did you experience?

The Journey towards Cultural Competence

Experience, as well as study, is required to understand the many subtleties of another culture; such information cannot be gleaned from a book. If we are truly committed to a journey towards cultural competence, we must take the time to immerse ourselves in other cultures—to learn as much as possible from those who appear to be different from us. This requires a willingness to be vulnerable and to allow others to see how little we really know.

Understanding another culture is a continuous process. The journey to cultural competence never ends; there is always something more to learn. A person can never know all there is to know about another culture. The purpose of this book is to challenge you to recognize how little you know, and to encourage you to commit to a lifelong learning process about similarities and differences between cultures and people. Let's begin the journey.

Differences Stand Out

When people talk about other cultures, they tend to describe the differences and not the similarities. This seems to be the way human beings are programmed. We are biologically geared to notice when things aren't the way we want them to be; incidents barely register when they match our expectations. Do you ever remember noticing that a room was the perfect temperature? Probably not. On the other hand, it probably registered immediately if you were too cold or too hot in a particular room. Noticing when expectations are not met encourages us to act. If the room is comfortable, we tend to enjoy the moment and we don't change what we are doing. However, if the room is uncomfortable, we will change some aspect of who we are or what we are doing, to improve our comfort level.

This concept extends to people. When we are invited to an event, often we inquire about the dress code so that we can blend in and not be perceived as different. We don't want to be noticed for being "out of line." When we interact with others, we notice how we are different much quicker than we recognize how we are the same. The differences separate us while the similarities help us form connections. It is vital to take the time to get beyond the differences and to find underlying ways to connect along the similarities. We will talk more about this in Chapter 15.

Kim and Sylvester's Experiences

Since we (Kim and Sylvester) became friends, we each have greatly extended our comfort zone by going into the culture of the other person. Kim was the first, traveling to Chicago from rural Pennsylvania, to visit Sylvester's home town. There were so many differences! She remembers the high level of stress and anxiety the first time she drove through the city of Chicago. When she became lost and sensed that she was not in a very good neighborhood, she was terrified. She could not understand Sylvester's cavalier attitude about her distress.

Being from the country, Kim had been taught that cities are scary places. She didn't mind driving through, but she sure didn't want to be lost in the city. All sorts of bad things could happen there. Although her fear and concerns were valid, Sylvester had a difficult time understanding them because of his level of comfort in that environment.

Now, contrast this with Sylvester's first experience in rural Pennsylvania. Kim's son wanted Sylvester to go with him outside to feed the dogs. It was nighttime so Kim turned on the floodlights on the back of the house. When Sylvester came back inside, he was visibly shaken by how dark it was outside. Being from the city, he had a message in his head that bad things happen in the country where there are no street lights after dark.

Because we both had a willingness to learn and stretch beyond what was familiar, we were able to push through our fears and expand our comfort zones. Actually, stretching your comfort zone is not enough; it is important to embrace the experience and learn from it. If during the encounter you are constantly judging, you are minimizing your ability to receive and process the information objectively. This does not lead to cultural competence; instead it further reinforces your desire to stay within your comfort zone.

Another amusing story relates to our attending each other's place of worship. The similarity is that both churches are Christian; that's where the similarity ends.

When Kim went to Sylvester's church, she was struck by the clapping, the dancing, and the shouting out in praise. Everyone was loud, happy, and dramatic. The choir sang joyous hymns in beautiful harmony without any sheet music. The pastor was doing something called "laying on of hands" and people were falling on the floor, their bodies in certain contortions. This was a very foreign experience for Kim.

On the other hand, when Sylvester attended Kim's church, he was amazed at how quiet and reverent everyone was. No one spoke a word during the pastor's sermon. No one spoke out of turn during the prayers. There was no exaltation, only introspection. No one stood unless it was time to sing. Everyone used sheet music, but the harmony was questionable. This was a very foreign experience for Sylvester.

However, we were both enriched by engaging and immersing ourselves in each other's culture.

Cultural Immersion/Pushing through the Fear

The best way to learn about another culture is to immerse yourself in it. Go to the area and live among the people. It's always best to have a guide, someone who can explain your experiences and advise you about how you are expected to behave. Several scenes from the movie, *Rush Hour*, illustrated some cultural issues that occurred between a black man, played by Chris Tucker, and an Asian, played by Jackie Chan. The movie was a comedy about an Asian-American attempting to blend into the African-American culture without a road map. Jackie Chan was operating without any understanding of the rules and expectations of the culture. Consequently, he made many mistakes that made for some hilarious comedy—particularly the bar scene and what happened while he was waiting for Mr. Tucker to return. However, in real life, this comical situation could have resulted in tragedy.

Whenever you find yourself in an unfamiliar culture, it is wise to humble yourself enough to ask how people want to be treated and what is polite and expected. While asking may seem a bit awkward and unusual, it is a very effective way to understand another culture.

A simple thing such as the seating positions of two couples riding in a car together can vary according to the culture. In certain cultures, one couple will sit in the front seats while the other couple will sit in the back. In other cultures, the men will occupy the front while the women will sit together in the back. And in other cultures, the couples will mix, the man from one couple sitting with the woman from the other couple. Rather than assuming your way is *the* way, ask the host what is proper. If you don't want to ask, just discretely follow the host's lead.

Having a different cultural experience can be either terrifying or enriching. Kim found that initially she was terrified. However, the more she immersed herself in the other culture and the more she pushed beyond her fear, the more comfortable she became.

While in Italy, Sylvester had a variety of cultural experiences that were enlightening. First, he experienced being out of the United States during the Fourth of July. It took him a while before it dawned on him that the American Independence Day did not exist in Italy. All day he expected to see backyard barbeques and fireworks.

Also while in Italy, he was introduced to another aspect of his own culture that he found somewhat shocking. Sylvester had never traveled outside of the United States. His experience with blacks was limited to black African-Americans. (Yes, Sylvester makes this distinction because he knows that some African-Americans may not be black.) Sylvester encountered Africans everyday while in Italy and his interactions with them were less than friendly.

He could not understand this because he thought he was still in his comfort zone, when in actuality he was not. He felt that being around black people would not be any different than what he was accustomed to, but was he ever mistaken! Although the Africans in Italy looked similar to Sylvester, they were from a different culture. Once Sylvester got to know some of them and began to learn about their culture, he developed a new perspective on blacks—one that he would never had experienced had he not left his comfort zone.

Kim remembers one of her first trips to Chicago, which was to attend Sylvester's graduation party. When she arrived, she knew no one, because Sylvester and his wife were not yet there. On top of that, she was the only Caucasian at the party. She felt quite frightened and uncomfortable. Interestingly, now she will attend events with Sylvester and his family and not even notice that she is the only Caucasian until well into the event. Over time a person's comfort level increases, when interacting with a different culture.

Statistics show that most people live and die within a 50-mile radius of where they were born.[1] Many people never leave the communities in which they live, not even for vacation. When they do vacation, often they visit the same place year after year. The obvious problem that this practice can create is a very strong sense of ethnocentrism. As children grow and develop, this ethnocentrism may affect their choice of colleges. Many times children may choose a college close to home because of their comfort level with the familiar.

Leaving One's Comfort Zone

People who never leave their comfort zone, never become aware of any possible differences. The world is seen through a very narrow view. When they encounter anything out of the ordinary, they often reject it because it doesn't fit their limited paradigm.

This was very cleverly demonstrated in the movie, *The Village*. The people who created this village started spreading myths about what was in the woods just beyond the village. The myths were created to keep the village people afraid so that they would never leave the village. The villagers believed these myths, incorporating them into their psyche, so that no one ever ventured out into the woods. There was no life or world beyond their small existence in the village. This is a very common practice for many people, who rarely venture beyond their comfort zone.

To be culturally sensitive, we must not judge people who choose to live their lives this way. If they want to stay within their comfort zone and never venture beyond it, that is their business. However, if we wish to become more culturally aware and accepting, then we are going to need to leave our comfort zone.

Leaving our comfort zone is not necessarily a physical act; we do not have to travel abroad. Leaving our comfort zone can be psychological. It can involve watching television shows, listening to radio broadcasts, and visiting web sites of alternative cultures. Sylvester has learned a great deal by leaving his comfort zone in this way. Understanding the views of a culture different from his is often difficult and he struggles to be objective. However, he manages to keep an open mind by simply saying that "this is different" as opposed to "this is wrong."

When you encourage employees to celebrate their culture while at work, you offer others an opportunity to share in that culture. Watching movies together, having weekly discussions, or having monthly cultural luncheons, are just some of the ways to offer employees the opportunity to leave their comfort zone. These activities will offer employees a peek into the cultures of their co-workers, which can lead to better camaraderie amongst the employees. A better understanding of another person's culture often leads to an appreciation and respect for that culture.

Sylvester remembers a story about young black men living in a group home in the south suburbs of Chicago. They were required to get up at six o'clock in the morning to make their beds, shower and dress, and have breakfast before they left for school. These young men would constantly complain about having to wake up that early in the morning. They believed that they should be able to sleep longer and make their beds when they got home from school. They had become so entrenched in their comfort zone that the staff decided to provide them with a different kind of experience.

These young black men were given the opportunity to take an overnight trip to a farm in a very rural area. While they were intrigued by the animals and how much work it took to run the farm, what really amazed them was that they were awakened at 4'oclock in the morning to accompany the teenagers who lived on the farm. The teenagers on the farm had two hours of chores to complete before preparing themselves for school—and then they walked several miles to school.

At the end of their school day they walked back home, did more chores, and completed their homework. Then they ate dinner and went to bed so that they could repeat it all over again the next day. When the young men from the group home observed this farming culture, they developed a new appreciation for their life. Leaving their comfort zone will frequently enlighten people, making them more objective and open-minded.

We all need to venture beyond the familiar. We need to let others know how little we actually know. We need to humble ourselves and learn from others. We need to open our mind to the fact that differences aren't bad. Differences can often open up possibilities that we wouldn't have been able to consider before.

Leaving your comfort zone will help you connect with other people in ways you never imagined. Go ahead. Take the risk. Read a book that you would not read. Listen to a type of music that you would not listen to. Eat a kind of food that you would not normally eat. Know it will be scary at first; but if you face your fear and do it anyway, then your comfort zone will expand, making more opportunities available to you. Thus you will enhance your life, as well as the lives of those you touch.

In the next chapter, we will discuss the compromising situations that can result from leaving one's comfort zone.

Compromising our Culture

As explained in the previous chapter, it is very important that we move beyond our comfort zone. This can be difficult because we may feel that we are not being true to who we are. We have a tendency to avoid going into new territory when we feel that we are compromising our culture. Our culture carries with it an unwritten credo that defines who we are and what we do. It is the road map that we live by, and deviating from this map can be very uncomfortable.

Compromising culture is another way of saying people fear the unknown and are resistant to change. We cling to what's familiar like a drowning man clings to a life preserver. It's a wonder that change occurs at all when we consider the pressure that our culture inflicts on anyone who thinks or acts differently. Those who are attempting to do things differently are admonished not to make waves by the cultural group to which they belong. On the other hand, the cultural group to which they seek to gain entry may try to block their entrance because it fears the effects of infiltration by an outsider.

Exclusion

The culture for the Augusta National Golf Club, which has hosted the Master's Tournament for many years, allowed only white males to become members. In September 1990, the first black member, Robert Townsend, was admitted. Ironically, 20 years earlier, a Mexican American golfer named Lee Trevino turned down membership to the Augusta National Golf Club and refused to play in the tournament in 1970 and 1971, stating that he felt uncomfortable in what remained a largely white, southern organization. Although the PGA has upgraded its membership standards to eliminate discrimination based on color, women are still not allowed to be members.

There are a myriad of other examples of exclusion. In 1955, when Rosa Parks refused to give up her seat on the bus to a white, fellow traveler, she forever changed the culture in America. Naturally, there was great resistance from Caucasians who feared that their culture would be compromised by allowing blacks certain privileges. But even blacks, while applauding Ms. Parks' courage, had their concerns; they were afraid of retaliation resulting from these new assertions of their rights.

Kim remembers that there was a big uproar at the thought of women being permitted to be firefighters on the front line during fires. Firemen didn't think that the women could handle it and feared that women would compromise their culture. Furthermore, many women didn't understand why a woman would want to enter an exclusively male-dominated profession. However, in 1973, Sandra Forcier became the first woman to be paid for fighting fires. She was hired as a Public Safety Officer with dual duties as a fire fighter and police officer. The following year, Judith Livers became the first woman to be hired for a strictly firefighting position.

Examples of Compromising Cultures

When the Roe vs. Wade Supreme Court Decision was made in 1973, it changed the culture of the entire United States, granting women the power to make decisions over their bodies and to terminate unwanted pregnancies. This is another example of compromising culture which has created a gaping chasm between pro-choice and pro-life proponents.

Another example of a compromising culture is President Clinton's "Don't Ask, Don't Tell" policy, which came into effect in 1993, allowing gays in the military. The military has always had a history of intolerance toward gays. Homosexual behavior was grounds for discharge. However, during wartime, this regulation became a problem because some men were using it to avoid military service, by claiming they were gay. In 1981, the Department of Defense issued a regulation on homosexuality, making homosexual status and conduct grounds for an honorable discharge. The 1993 "Don't Ask, Don't Tell" policy was considered a compromise. As long as gays didn't engage in homosexual activity, the military was not permitted to investigate their sexual orientation.

Kim works with a company in Pennsylvania that has totally restructured its corporate climate—changing from a traditionally autocratic leadership to one of total quality management. This transition met with much resistance from employees who had become comfortable being told what to do. Management also became uncomfortable because it believed that the employees were taking advantage of their newly found power, and were not keeping management informed. Management's knee jerk reaction was to revert back to the days of autocratic leadership.

The Majority Corporate Culture

It is important to understand that in this next section, we are not criticizing the majority corporate culture. The trends we have observed do not come from outright sexism, racism, ageism or any other "isms." Most of the systems in place are not conscious, but simply a result of cultural indoctrination. We are attempting to assist those with strong cultural lenses to take off their glasses and view the world from another perspective—to truly embrace all that diversity has to offer. Are you willing? Are you ready?

The majority corporate culture may view including women and minorities who retain their own cultural identities into upper management as a compromise of their culture. In many companies, attention to diversity issues has definitely enhanced the hiring of women and people of color. These groups are also receiving more promotions than ever before. However, there is still an unspoken rule that makes it difficult for them to be promoted unless they compromise their culture. In order to be seriously considered for promotion, women are expected to make decisions that compromise their family values, while people of color are subtly encouraged to blend more into the corporate culture. Thus, the corporate majority can maintain its culture at the expense of the other cultures.

This is similar to the "Don't Ask, Don't Tell" policy in the military. As long as minorities conform to the norms and values of the majority culture, then that majority will compromise to the point of allowing them entrance.

The business world is constantly changing; supply and demand are always fluctuating. In the last five years there has been a major influx of the Hispanic and Latino population into the United States. This growth in the Spanish-speaking population has caused businesses to stand up and take notice. While it is prudent for companies to accommodate a new and growing population, some companies may feel pressure to compromise their culture in order to serve this new audience. They may avoid making any adjustments in order to maintain their comfort level, sacrificing profits as a result.

Loyalty to the Culture

Cliques and close relationships develop in most businesses since people work together for years. These relationships create a mini-culture whose members become comfortable within it.

Because companies are generally looking to grow and expand, new employees—whose character and physical make up may not coincide with the established culture—will inevitably be introduced into the company. Members of the established corporate culture may find the qualities and characteristics of the new employees interesting and exciting. They may desire to spend time with the new employees but are reluctant to do so because of fear that they would be compromising their culture by cavorting with "outsiders." This hesitance to show acceptance of others can cause dissension within a company.

Isolated employees feel the separation most when office parties are held. However, office parties can be used to give people opportunities to connect with others, without feeling the pressure of compromising their culture. Through games and other group activities, employees who would otherwise remain disconnected, can come together and work in a fun and pleasurable atmosphere.

In politics, most blacks are expected to be Democrats since the Democratic Party is viewed to be more in line with the needs and desires of the black population. Over the years, blacks in politics who have not been democrats have received some negative attention because of their affiliation with another culture. This dates back to pre-civil rights. If a white person befriended a black person, they were often referred to as a "nigger lover." Correspondingly, if blacks were accepted by whites they were called "Uncle Toms." It's this kind of backlash that influences people to "stay with their own kind."

When we feel that we are a part of an institution, we strive to be loyal to it, as well as support it in all that we say and do. Our actions and choices represent the culture to which we belong—and are often predictable. We acclimate to these cultural expectations, which become a natural way of life for us. Anything outside the norm is often scrutinized and frowned upon, causing suffering to many relationships.

Suffering as a Result of Culture

Never is this more true than among religious groups. We have only to look to the Middle East to see how the Holy Wars have torn entire nations apart. Because religions are completely based on faith, there is no way to substantiate or refute them. Yet people kill and die for these beliefs.

In some relationships, one partner will change his or her religion so that the couple can worship together and raise their children in one faith. We know people who converted to Catholicism, the Jewish faith, and the Muslim faith when they were married. Without exception, these people had to contend with the criticism of friends and family who accused them of compromising their culture.

Many heads of companies strongly believe in "hiring their own." This is the practice of staying within one's own culture when choosing an employee. While this practice is widely accepted and may have some validity, when does the practice of hiring the best person come into play?

Affirmative Action was introduced in 1965 by President Johnson as a method of redressing discrimination that had persisted, despite civil rights laws and constitutional guarantees. This policy was enacted to bring about equity in hiring practices. Focusing in particular on education and jobs, Affirmative Action policies required that active measures be taken to ensure that blacks and other minorities enjoyed the same opportunities as whites for promotions, salary increases, career advancement, school admissions, scholarships, and financial aid.

From the outset, Affirmative Action was envisioned as a temporary remedy that would end once there was a "level playing field" for all Americans. However, Affirmative Action received a great deal of negative attention and feedback. In 1978 reverse discrimination became a concern. This fear of compromising one's culture continues to influence the hiring practices of many managers.

Healing the Separation

Much of what we know about our culture is handed down to us from elders. Some cultures teach hatred, which may encourage people to disassociate with members of a group that would be of benefit to them.

In the movie Malcolm X, Malcolm was trained and taught to hate whites. As he grew older, hatred for whites was reinforced in him. He went about his life denouncing whites, never compromising his cultural beliefs until he began to understand that this sweeping indictment was not justified. He then publicly admitted his bias, as well as his change in position, and became a more well-rounded person. While some applauded his transformation, others in his culture thought he "sold out." Like Malcolm, we will all have the opportunity to evaluate our beliefs in our culture, and the question is, will we take it?

There are times when our outmoded beliefs and actions just don't work any longer. Many businesses today still encourage the "good ol' boy" mentality. There are still instances of white males not willing to work with women or people of color. These outmoded beliefs and actions can limit the growth of an organization. If we continue to hold the belief that women are not strong or that people of color are not smart, we could overlook the next Oprah Winfrey or the next Russell Simmons, music mogul and CEO of Rush Communications, Inc.

Many of us don't evaluate our own culture objectively. We are more likely to examine other cultures and determine what is wrong with them than we are to look into our own culture. Evaluating our own culture means that we have doubt. It feels like compromising. However, we look in the mirror each and everyday, not because we want to compromise our looks but because we want to be sure that we are being who we want to be. We make adjustments because we believe that they will move us closer to personal acceptance, which is what we are striving for.

On the other side of compromising are people who are honestly attempting to connect with a different cultural group but are blocked admission because the group fears outsiders and compromising their culture. What can a person do when this occurs? Gracefully respect the boundaries as defined by the group. Remain on the fringe and perhaps attempt to befriend one person from the group. Sometimes all that is needed to be accepted is the endorsement of just one member of the group.

Cultural compromise is more of a fallacy than a reality. There is an expression that says, "God made one race—the human race. Man made racism." Our commonalities lie in our humanness. Our differences make things more interesting. They should not separate and divide us.

The only boundaries that exist between people are the walls that they themselves construct out of fear. The answer is not in building higher, thicker walls but in tearing down the walls that keep us apart, and encouraging communication that will assist us in getting to know one another. Encouraging objectivity and unity is not about compromising; it's about coming together so that we can all benefit. A unified group is a stronger and more successful group.

In the next chapter we will discuss communication, with its accompanying challenges and complications.

Communication

"People fear each other because people don't know each other. People don't know each other because they don't communicate with each other."

—Dr. Martin Luther King, Jr.

Communication is the common denominator among people. However, it frequently results in misunderstandings because of the differences in the way we communicate and the different meanings of our words. This chapter provides a blueprint for improving communication within your company.

All companies depend on communication—the successful ones as well as the struggling ones. Communication is the medium for interpersonal relationships and group interactions. The problem is that communication is highly influenced by culture; the way a person communicates is a direct product of his or her culture.

A company on the road to managing diversity needs to understand the communication nuances of the cultural groups represented by its employees, its suppliers, and its clientele. Creating an environment where people understand the importance of communication and its strong cultural influence is very helpful. People will begin to ask and learn about communication differences. This will, in turn, help them become more culturally aware. Communicating across cultures is a valued ability in this information age.

Cultural Context

Anthropologist Edward Hall developed the concept of cultural context.[1] He explains that different cultures fall somewhere along the cultural context continuum, ranging from low to high context. Context, in this instance, is defined as the interrelated conditions in which something exists—the social and cultural conditions that surround and influence the life of an individual, an organization, or a community.

In a high context culture, the circumstances surrounding an interaction are taken into account. Body language, tonal inflections, and facial expressions are all factored into the equation. In contrast, a low context culture filters out these extraneous variables and focuses instead solely on the objective facts that are presented. High contexts are not valued more than low contexts—they are simply different. Most workplaces have employees whose cultural contexts vary; this can present communication challenges unless there is an understanding of these differences.

For example, high context interactions require time. Trust must be established and relationships developed. Many factors are taken into consideration, such as personal needs, individual differences, the weather, and holidays. Low context interactions, on the other hand, tend to be faster and more efficient. Relationships begin and end quickly; verbal messages are direct; change occurs quickly; and a strict schedule for doing things is typically followed.

In general, females tend to favor high context interactions, while males are drawn to low context interactions. People who live in rural areas generally favor high context interactions, while people from urban environments seem to favor low context exchanges. At work, social workers tend to be high context, while computer programmers are low context. According to Hall's research, the United States falls into the medium-low area on the cultural context continuum.

Neither context culture is preferable. What is most valuable in the workplace is that people understand their own tendencies, realize how their personal context preference affects their ability to work with others, and make the necessary adjustments to work cohesively with others.

An executive who is forming a work group should have both high and low context individuals involved for a well-rounded approach to the situation. It is also advisable for team members to understand this combination of high and low context so that they can appreciate the resulting balanced view rather than becoming frustrated by the difference.

While it may be more comfortable working with individuals who share our particular cultural context orientation, the drawbacks are that we are only looking at a problem from one vantage point, which limits our ability to see a variety of potential solutions.

Hall's Categories of Human Activity

Hall developed five categories of human activity that are critical to understanding cultural differences in organizations: association, interaction, territoriality, temporality, and learning.[2]

Association involves our preferred way of relating to each other and how we form relationships. In the United States, it is unthinkable for a person to not have free will to choose their own life partner. Of course family and friends may attempt to influence a person's decision, but it is generally agreed that only an individual can determine who their life partner will be. However, in other cultures, such as in certain parts of India, the parents have the responsibility of choosing a husband or wife for their children. (Before making any judgments about this, remember the divorce rate in the United States.)

Interaction involves both the verbal and non-verbal ways in which we communicate with each other, including but not limited to: gestures, facial expressions, tone of voice, volume and cadence of speech, eye contact, sense of humor, and sensitivity to certain topics of conversation.

An example of an interaction difference that Kim was particularly struck by was in Sylvester's home, watching several of his friends playing cards. Playing cards at Sylvester's home looked very different from the way that was familiar to her. Kim had frequently witnessed her parents and their friends playing pinochle. They used the quiet tones of a typical social conversation, with an occasional exclamation of triumph when a set of partners won a particular hand.

In contrast, around Sylvester's card table, a game of Bid Whist involved a lot of yelling. People stood up and puffed out their chest to emphasize their point, often making comments that were not polite, to say the least. Kim feared that a physical altercation might take place. She later learned, however, that "trash talking" and displays of intimidation are an integral part of the communication that occurs during a card game in certain cultures. It's all part of the fun!

Territoriality is defined as the amount of space one is comfortable having during certain interactions. A number of variables influence this factor: the type of relationship; the size of the other person; the other person's gender, appearance, personal hygiene, manners, etc.

Culture is a factor known to significantly influence the perceived appropriate distance of personal space. In the United States the typical distance for a casual conversation between two people is approximately one and a half to two feet. Some Asian cultures are known to be comfortable with much closer personal space.

When Kim was in Australia, she accompanied a woman to a local Chinese take-out restaurant. Kim hadn't noticed any discomfort with personal space issues in Australia, until she went to this restaurant. Despite the fact that there was a fairly large open space in the ordering section, the people in line were standing so close to each other that they were almost touching. Kim definitely noticed this, as people are programmed to notice differences more than similarities.

Temporality is defined as the way a person views time. Some cultures, such as Americans, count time by the seconds that are marked by a clock. In Chapter 1 Sylvester already mentioned that this is his personal bias. Other cultures, Native Americans for example, view time as a rhythm or cycles of growth. Even within the predominant American culture, there is a wide variance in how people measure time.

We have trained companies all over the country. One of our standing jokes when in Philadelphia is that Philadelphians are on their own schedule. (Please forgive this stereotyping.) Even though our training sessions begin at 9 a.m., people will often arrive at 10 a.m., believing they are on time. Some people believe they are not *really* tardy if someone comes into the training after they themselves have arrived. This temporality may not be specific to Philadelphia but may be accepted in other larger cities, particularly when traffic can be unpredictable. However discrepancies over measuring and assessing time can cause tremendous conflict between people.

Learning is defined as the knowledge and skills that are valued within a particular culture, and their methods of transmission. What is considered necessary learning in a rural culture is very different from that of an urban culture. Consider the simple example of transportation. In most rural environments, students must pass a driver's education class before they are allowed to graduate high school. However, in the cities it is more important for students to learn how to read the bus, subway, or train schedules.

Cultural Trends

Research has shown certain cultural trends among various groups of people. We are often reluctant to share this information because it can lead to the perpetuation of certain stereotypes. However, when working cross culturally, having a certain understanding of collective cultural trends can be helpful in developing a dialogue—until more information is acquired about the individual. Remember, there are more differences within a particular cultural group than there are between groups.

We will summarize the available research as it relates to four particular cultural and ethnic groups in the United States:[3]

- White Americans
- Asian-Americans
- Hispanics
- African-Americans

When we hold diversity workshops, we generally ask participants who identify with one of these particular cultural groups to decide how much of the generalities are true for them. What often occurs is that they can relate to some, but never to all, of the generalities. Let's see what's true for you.

White Americans have been shown to have an "I" rather than a "we" orientation to the world. They value individualism and competitiveness. They perceive the nuclear, rather than the extended family, as a family unit. They have a preference for tradition, order and control, and low emotion. Conversation is generally direct and polite. There is an insistence on "standard English." Time is measured by the clock, with a value on promptness. There is a preference for linear, as opposed to circuitous, problem solving methods. Life events are rarely viewed within a cultural context.

Asian-Americans demonstrate strong family connections, with a high respect for authority. They generally do not like arguments or aggressive behavior. Public reprimands are distasteful. Their tendency is toward modesty, reserve, and self-control. There is patience and respect for silence. Privacy is important. They value tradition and history. Their culture is highly structured, with many expectations concerning certain behaviors. They tend to address others with titles, viewing the use of first names as a show of disrespect. Asian-Americans tend to laugh when embarrassed and rarely engage in spontaneous behavior.

Hispanics value unity and interdependence among the members of their family—family being the extended family. There is an expectation that extended family members will assist in the care of the young and the elderly. Hispanics respect tradition—the traditional family and social roles. They have a flexible sense of time. During conversation, there is an intensity of emotion and expression, often with physical closeness and touching. Hispanics prefer a field-dependent, socially oriented, hands on approach to learning, as opposed to classroom instruction.

African-Americans have a "we" rather than "I" view of the world. In conversation, they use a call/response style, meaning that the listener often adds encouragers or affirmations during the speaker's comments. They prefer story telling and connecting when making a point. African-Americans generally display intense emotion and expression when speaking. They avoid direct eye contact when listening but use direct eye contact when speaking. There are strong "in group" tendencies and rules of conduct that result in perceptions of disrespect when outsiders attempt to ingratiate themselves into the group without permission. Blacks also prefer a field-dependent, socially oriented, hands on approach to learning.

Kim remembers an incident when, as a social worker, she was speaking to the African-American father of a child who had just been placed in foster care. Many of the other women in the office perceived this man to be hostile and potentially physically aggressive. They based these assumptions on his behavior of looking off in the distance whenever someone talked to him, and then making intense eye contact when he responded. To these women he felt threatening. In fact, this man was demonstrating his culture's behavior of appropriate eye contact. Without this understanding, great misunderstanding can ensue.

Miscommunication

There is often a great deal of miscommunication within organizations. Because we don't take time to understand communication from an objective point of view, we often misinterpret what an individual is really trying to say.

Sylvester recalls working in an environment where he was a supervisor; one of his staff was Hispanic while the rest were black. In meetings, many of the black staff would often become agitated with the Hispanic employee because they believed she spoke in a degrading way toward them. Upon further examination of this problem, Sylvester discovered that the problem was in the way she used certain words. For instance, whenever the Hispanic employee gave information, she ended her statement with "OK?" The black employees felt that she was questioning their ability to understand her. The fact was that she did want to make sure that they understood her, because she wasn't confident of her English. So their perception of her intent was correct but the motivation they assigned that intent was wrong.

Positional Communication

When working in an organization, we readily accept information and directives from our manager more easily than our co-workers. The problem just mentioned would probably have been perceived differently if the Hispanic employee had been the manager. The position or status of a person plays a big part in our accepting the person's communication. Who says it is just as important as what is said.

Trusting the people who provide the information is even more important. If we have a good relationship with them, and our trust level is fairly high, then we are more likely to receive what they are saying. If, on the other hand, we have a poor relationship, then we will probably seek confirmation from someone else within the organization whom we do trust.

Effective Communication

Imagine a company where there is no ability to communicate verbally. Would it be more difficult to work effectively together? Many would contend that it would, but the fact is, in most companies, verbal communication is not used effectively; often it creates more problems.

Let's say that a male employee has a problem with the boss. The boss always encourages employees to talk openly when there are issues so that they can work them out. This employee doesn't really want to talk to the boss, so he shares his concerns with co-workers with whom he feels more comfortable. One of the reasons he feels more comfortable is because his co-workers share his feelings. In his conversations with them, the employee only gets communication that further justifies his feelings, making him become more and more disenchanted with the boss. By the time he decides to speak with the boss, he is so firm in his beliefs that objectivity is no longer present—all a result of verbal communication.

It is important to nurture an understanding of communication. Encourage employees to really seek to understand everything that is being communicated in conversations. Assign certain people who are more skilled in communication to arbitrate misunderstandings. Do not ignore communication challenges; that will only lead to more separation. Always seek to improve communication; it will really improve the overall environment within a company.

In the next chapter we will discuss how communication is enhanced when we are able to connect through our similarities while appreciating our differences.

Connecting Through Similarities and Celebrating Differences

"Once you identify yourself with a particular population, members of that group are transformed in your mind from 'them' to 'us.'"

—Sondra Theiderman, Ph.D.

On the surface, when we (Kim and Sylvester) first met, we couldn't have been any more different. Kim was a white, 36 year-old woman, married and raising teenaged boys in rural Pennsylvania. Sylvester was a black, 35 year-old man, single and raising a preadolescent daughter in south suburban Chicago. Kim owned her country home; Sylvester rented his city apartment. Given these demographics, there is no way we should ever have met, let alone become best friends. How did it happen?

Similarities

How did we connect? We were in a two-year training program together, to become instructors for the William Glasser Institute, so that we could teach Choice Theory, Reality Therapy, Lead Management, and Quality School ideas to people who wanted to learn them. There were eight people in the class—five of whom already knew each other. The three remaining people who didn't know anyone in the group—Sylvester, Kim and Ellen—came together due to a similar need for connection.

We (Kim and Sylvester) further connected based on the work we did: we both functioned as the heads of training programs for child welfare agencies. In addition, we both had an interest in counseling and spiritual growth, and we both liked to sing—one professionally and the other karaoke. As we got to know each other, we learned that we also had similar value systems, despite the fact that we were raised very differently.

These similarities formed a firm basis for our friendship, but what sustained it was an appreciation of our differences. We don't shy away from our differences; in fact, we embrace them so that we can grow as individuals. Learning not only to identify our similarities, but also to appreciate our differences, goes a long way in establishing quality relationships.

Recently, Kim attended the "Body Worlds" exhibit at a Chicago museum. This was a fabulous exhibit of actual cadavers that had been preserved to educate museum goers as to the workings of the human body. If we simply look at the physiological similarities of humans, they far outweigh our individual differences. For the most part we all walk upright on two legs, eat with our mouths, and manipulate tools with our hands. We have the same number of bones in our bodies and similar muscular systems. We all breathe in air and expel carbon monoxide. Our digestive tracts are similar. Once our skin is removed, we can easily see how our circular systems are the same.

Dr. Sondra Thiederman in her book, *Making Diversity Work*, states, "Eighty-five percent of genetic differences between people is not between races or ethnic groups but between individuals within those groups. This means that members of two racial groups can be more alike than members of the same group."[1] Margaret Mead, in *A Rap on Race,* claims that boats are responsible for racial distinctions. She says that if everyone had to emigrate from Africa by foot, the variations in skin color would be so miniscule as to be of no consequence.[2]

The similarities within the human race are overwhelming, far outweighing any differences such as the ones we mentioned between Kim and Sylvester. However, if Kim and Sylvester had only looked at the differences between them and had not learned to appreciate them, they probably would never have gotten to a place where they could even see the similarities.

An Exercise in Culture Shock

When we do our training in Cultural Awareness, we include an activity that simulates culture shock. The actual purpose of this exercise is unbeknownst to the training participants. They believe that they are simply playing a new card game. However, as the activity progresses, participants actually experience many of the thoughts, feelings, and behaviors of someone in the uncomfortable situation of culture shock.

At the end of the exercise, when processing what had occurred, participants were often surprised by how vicious and mean they had become. When card players who didn't "belong" entered a new group and began to operate as if they understood that group's protocol—when in reality they had it all wrong—the original members of the group became angry. They attempted to bully the new people into compliance with their group norms.

Sometimes the newcomers fought back, attempting to gain a place for themselves; but often they acquiesced to the group they were attempting to join. Newcomers experienced fear, uncertainty, disconnection, and helplessness. Conversely, the original members of the group were often intolerant and overbearing. They had derogatory thoughts about the newcomers, such as: "They are just stupid and don't get it." "What's wrong with them?" "Why can't they just adapt and do it the way everyone else does?" It is natural for those of us who know the rules, to feel that others who don't follow them are wrong. We judge them, because we are "clear" that we are right.

There is one thing that has never happened, in all our training experiences, during this particular activity. People have never sat down and attempted to join together based upon their similarities. They were all playing cards; they all had the same number of cards in each hand; they all wanted to win. Despite these similarities everyone focused on the differences, resulting in separation rather than connection.

Why Do We Focus on Differences?

In chapter one, we defined culture. Though this seems simple, it isn't. Oftentimes it is difficult to define culture, because culture is such an ever-present part of our life. It's similar to asking fish to define water. We often don't recognize culture on a conscious level; we just live it.

When we encounter something or someone who is different, we quickly identify that difference because it feels uncomfortable. We then, almost immediately, find ways to separate ourselves because it's not part of our culture. We like similarities; they feel right. Differences, on the other hand, are uncomfortable—and they are more apparent. Since they will be noticed, it is important to learn how to appreciate our differences.

How to Get to the Similarities

The beginning chapters of this book were written to help everyone—majority and minorities alike—develop an understanding and empathy for what the other group experiences. It is difficult to reach any connection without understanding.

Many systems in the United States, including many corporations, unfairly favor the majority culture, without even being aware. Many white men who consider themselves to be fair, simply don't have an understanding of the systems that exist to help them succeed, while leaving women and minorities at a great disadvantage. The majority culture needs to understand and recognize these systems. This can be challenging because these systems are so ingrained in our culture that they usually go unnoticed.

Women and members of minority cultures also need to understand that many well-meaning people make unintentional sexist, racist, and ageist mistakes. They simply don't know another way. This is especially true of people who don't embrace diversity. How can they be more sensitive to others if they haven't taken the time to gain a better, objective understanding of them?

The majority culture can gain a better understanding of the minority culture by providing opportunities, both formal and informal, for discussions centered around these issues. Members of the majority culture must be willing to hear the minorities' accusations with objectivity and understanding. They should not take the accusations personally but instead should view them as valid, genuine, and absolutely true from the perspective of the woman or minority.

It is difficult for members of the majority culture to understand the experience of women and people of color. Because they have always enjoyed privilege, they can't possibly understand the reality of those who don't. Even if a white man comes from an impoverished background, he still has advantages not available to people of color. While it may be difficult for the majority group to accept this fact, only when this disparity is understood and accepted, can we begin to move forward.

Minorities who have experienced a lack of power and privilege their entire lives, have difficulty explaining how they feel to those in power. This is like inmates in prison complaining to a correctional officer that they don't like their accommodations. Even though you, as an individual, may not be a person who wields your power over others, you are still identified by minorities as a member of the dominant oppressive culture. It is difficult for them to trust and confide in you.

Members of the majority culture must therefore take the first step because they are the ones with the power. Women and minorities need to feel safe and secure in the workplace. They need to feel that their words and concerns will be heard and not be used against them. They need to develop trust, which will not happen overnight.

When women and minorities perceive a new awareness in the dominant culture of their companies, they need to accept this openness as genuine and begin to trust that there is a possibility for improvement. They must begin to actively disclose their thoughts and concerns regarding inequities at work. While terrifying for both the manager and the employee, if all parties involved have an open mind, this can be the first step toward equity within the organization. Establishing trust can be difficult; it will require sharing and risk taking. When both sides are prepared to do this, the process can begin. The solution to connecting through similarities lies with both sides.

Companies can structure certain times for employees to find things in common with their co-workers. This can happen at the start of a business meeting, during staff development training, or during an informal company gathering. Furthermore, certain games can be played that enhance connections among people. One of our personal favorites is "two truths and a lie." Each person takes a turn sharing three pieces of information about him or herself—the more outrageous the better. Two pieces of information are true while one is a lie. Everyone playing the game guesses which is the lie. After everyone has guessed, the person whose turn it is shares which is the lie. Then the next person shares his or her three pieces of information until everyone has had a turn. It is a fun way to get to know interesting things about co-workers that wouldn't ordinarily be discussed.

Cultural Competence is a Journey, Not a Destination

"Cultural competence" is a term used to denote a person who has mastered the art of relating to a variety of different cultural groups. We are not in favor of this phrase because it seems to imply a certain finality to cultural competence, as if there is an end to cultural experience.

Becoming culturally competent is a lifetime journey, not a destination. If you believe you have arrived at the end of this journey, then you are mistaken. Studying culture and becoming more adept at navigating within different cultures is something that can always be improved upon. There is always more to learn. The real success is developing a desire and willingness to continue to learn. Though you will never learn all there is to know about every culture, you can position yourself to be more objective in receiving information from other cultures.

If your company is on the cutting edge, then you probably are experiencing an influx of employees from different cultural backgrounds. There may be more women, more people of color, a greater percentage of older workers, more workers with disabilities, and more gay employees in your workplace. Management and staff must work toward understanding the various cultures that exist within the company, so that a comfort level can be achieved when managing cultural differences and clashes. It is difficult, if not impossible, to function effectively in a culturally rich environment if these cultural differences are ignored. We understand that embracing diversity can be uncomfortable in the beginning, but understanding our similarities and appreciating our differences will only lead to a more well-rounded work force in the end.

We clearly do our employees a disservice whenever we fail to honor their cultural preferences. We create injustices whenever we judge our co-workers from our firm place of cultural righteousness and ethnocentrism. Becoming skilled in interacting cross-culturally is a process that requires a great deal of time, willingness, and patience. This must be a course to which the entire company is committed. People must be prepared to explore unknown territory. They must also become comfortable with being wrong, as frequent mistakes and misunderstandings will occur.

Celebrating Differences

In order to celebrate differences, we must have a clear understanding of the benefits of diversity. Since the beginning of time, men and women have attempted to create partnerships, lives, and families together. It didn't take John Gray's book, *Men are from Mars; Women are from Venus,* for couples to realize the significant differences between men and women.[3]

We aren't saying that couples have it all figured out, but they must recognize the value in these differences because they continue to get together and work at staying together. This is usually accomplished by establishing similarities in terms of common goals and life experiences—such as raising their children or accomplishing certain socioeconomic goals together. They recognize the strengths each of them brings to their relationship, and they value the differences.

The same process needs to be deliberately discussed at work. There must be some agreement, among management and staff, on the vision and mission of the company. Disagreeing about the "how" is acceptable, but the "what" should be clear, understood, and agreed upon by all employees. The company's mission and vision lay the foundation for similarities among employees. The common vision becomes the focus of all employees, and can be referred to as the common area of agreement whenever there is a problem between two parties.

Once the vision is agreed upon, it is important to encourage employees to discuss different approaches to achieve it. Providing a forum for public recognition and appreciation of differences will help minorities value themselves; at the same time it will help the majority culture understand the importance and value of diversity in the workplace.

To celebrate differences, individuals must be strong enough to identify, label, and confront any behavior that is culturally insensitive. Any stereotyping, prejudice, and discrimination must be brought out into the open and be confronted, since these are damaging to relationships in the workplace. This is a delicate process, requiring a great deal of pre-teaching and discussion. Helping people understand how destructive negative statements and feelings can be may sound easy; but when these feelings have been a part of them for as long as they can remember, people can have difficulty releasing them. However, anything that occurs in the workplace that separates people must be identified and openly discouraged. This will be discussed further in Chapter 20—Making the Commitment.

In the next chapter, we will discuss why diversity at work is so critically important.

Diversity at Work

"According to the teachings of the Baha'i Faith, 'associate with each other, think of each other, and be like a rose garden. Anyone who goes into a rose garden will see various roses, white, pink, yellow, red, all growing together and replete with adornment. Each one accentuates the beauty of the other. If we were all of one color, the garden would be monotonous to the eye . . . But when the colors are varied . . . white, pink, yellow, red . . . therein lies the greatest beauty.' Therefore, I hope that you will be like a rose garden. Although different in colors, yet praise be to God!—you receive rays from the same sun."

—Brenda Altuna[1]

If culture is so important to every aspect of our lives, then why do we ignore cultural differences in society and at work? Why do we try to act as if cultural differences don't matter?

Kim remembers sitting in a hotel lounge with people who were having a conversation about racial differences. One white man said to a black man, "Hey, I've been talking to you all this time and I didn't even notice you were black!" This comment was insulting to the man who was proud of being black; his skin color was a big part of his identity. The white man was probably just attempting to connect with him by letting him know that color wasn't important to him. There are times when, in an effort to avoid the perception of racism, we may dismiss the idea of race consciousness. But it's difficult to believe that someone can spend time talking face-to-face with a person of dark skin color and not "notice" that obvious difference.

Why Rock the Boat?

Now that you understand something about culture, the question becomes, why should you care? You run your company and believe that everything is fine. Everyone seems to get along well together. Some whites may even go out to eat with people of color at lunchtime. People of different races and ethnicities may socialize together after work. Your employees are just one big happy family, right?

Guess again. What happens among your employees when a critical situation develops? You know the situations we mean . . . the ones that create polar opposite sides along racial lines—events like the Rodney King incident, O.J. Simpson's acquittal, and most recently the treatment of New Orleans during Hurricane Katrina There are going to be differences of opinion, which is expected; but if during times of crisis and high stress, your employees begin dividing themselves based on gender, race, religion, or some other aspect of culture, you may indeed have a problem.

In most areas of the United States, there is still a great deal of work to do towards healing relationships between the races. Injustices perpetrated against any group will bring about anger. Women, people of color, certain religious groups, as well as other groups, have suffered injustices for hundreds, even thousands of years. It is natural that anger has built up.

Developing a sensitivity and understanding of people who are not members of the majority culture is the first step to healing. But to really improve relations, you must develop a set of cultural skills and use your cultural radar to locate incidents of inequities. If you are serious about masterfully managing diversity at work, then we have a lot to do. So let's get started!

The first question that arises is probably, why should we do this? Why now? Why make a concerted effort to increase the diversity among the workforce? If we initiate a diversity program, won't that bring up issues that are better left alone? Won't talking about issues just bring problems to the forefront? Won't that just produce more headaches? Isn't it better to have people who get along? Isn't it to our advantage to hire people who think and act just like us? There sure would be fewer headaches, wouldn't there?

Competition

In today's global economy, without an intensely diverse workforce, your company will be quickly surpassed by your competition. Demographics suggest that the number of minority cultures in this country is quickly growing. This means that in order to stay competitive, it is important to meet the demands of new and expanding consumer groups. What better way to do this than to employ members of that group? Diverse consumers will be attracted to your company because they will feel comfortable with your employees, and your employees will understand the consumers.

If your workforce does not understand the culture of the consumers or feels uncomfortable when facing them, your company will be unsuccessful in attracting different consumer groups. The white middle-class majority certainly does not have all the answers for all the people in the United States, let alone the entire globe. You must begin to develop and embrace the mindset that members of minority groups bring knowledge, skills, and abilities that will enhance your company's ability to compete in the global market. You must begin to recognize the value that diversity brings.

And just who are these minorities? Females, blacks, Latinos, Asians, Native Americans, homosexuals, bisexuals, people with disabilities, and members of different religious groups, just to name a few. Many individuals belonging to these co-cultures will be able to provide valuable insights into the marketplace.

Of course, there are the obvious language issues. In the United States, Spanish is spoken by more and more households. If you do any business with the Spanish-speaking population, you will need Spanish-speaking people in your workforce.

If you want to market to people of color, it would be useful to have insight into their needs and decision-making process when making purchases. Who better to know these than another person of color? Did you know that females make more buying decisions in the United States than males? How many women do you employ in positions where they can influence your marketing strategies? Is it possible that they may be able to market to other women more effectively than the male executives who are currently running your ad campaigns?

Moving Beyond Stereotypes

When adding diversity for the reasons just discussed, you must be careful not to think in a stereotypical fashion. Do not give Spanish-speaking employees only Spanish-speaking accounts. They may be seeking to expand their horizons beyond the cultural group from whence they came. If minorities become stereotyped and consequently pigeonholed, they could develop resentment and leave your employ.

Remember that individuals bring with them their unique cultural influence. Some of these differences may intuitively be viewed as bad for business. They are the ones that are generally not in line with the mainstream corporate American culture. However, we recommend that you step back and ask yourself, what is your ultimate goal and business objective? Can you still accomplish that objective while allowing for individual expression of cultural nuances?

Up until now, people who did not belong to the majority culture had to assimilate or acculturate to the mainstream in order to attain economic power and middle class status. However, it is no longer realistic or advisable to expect your employees to acculturate to the predominant culture of your company. Such assimilation results in unhappy, disgruntled employees who resent giving up a part of who they are to work for you. Today there are enough companies successfully managing diversity that women and people of color can resist the pressure to assimilate, thus retaining some of their diversity and uniqueness.

Avoiding Diversity

Diversity exists all around us; so why are some companies avoiding it? Mainly because of a desire for comfort. Many employers want to achieve profits in a comfortable environment, which oftentimes means having people around who are very similar to them.

Hip-Hop is a fast growing culture with a great deal of influence. A large percentage of the entertainment industry's revenue comes from record and video sales of the Hip-Hop culture. Although most companies understand this, some are not willing to hire people who represent this cultural group, because management is not comfortable with them. What ultimately happens is that consumers take their business somewhere where they feel represented, and consequently, more comfortable.

Years ago, when Sylvester did job development for a social service agency, he was informed by one manager that employees were hired based on the demographics of customers within the community. He believed that if the customers who visited his store felt represented, they would be more apt to return. At another time, Sylvester held a discussion with a group of teenagers concerning teenage unemployment. They discussed their desire to earn money but not to work. They shared their feelings about not taking minimum wage jobs. As Sylvester listened to these teenagers, he began to have a different view of them, and developed an understanding of how diversity in the workplace has made an impact on society.

Many of the teenagers were concerned that a large number of Hispanics were working in jobs that previously had been reserved for them. They felt that this was not fair. Sylvester asked them if they understood why the hiring of Hispanics had increased. They didn't know; they just knew that it was "wrong." People who don't understand diversity will often take offense to it because it just doesn't feel right. Sylvester explained to them how the demographics in the country were changing, and how many businesses were attempting to accommodate these changes through their hiring practices. As they continued to discuss this matter, the teenagers began to understand.

The Benefits of Diversity

Sometimes companies have views similar to these teenagers. They believe that adding diversity to their workforce would be wrong or unfair, and therefore, don't do it. This is why we stress the importance of communication within your organization. Employees are not necessarily against change; they just want to be informed and possibly be afforded an opportunity to contribute to it. With understanding comes success.

The first level of understanding has to come from management. Management's appreciation and acceptance of diversity within the organization, permeates throughout the company. You might ask how does management display appreciation and acceptance of diversity?

Let's look to the world of sports. Many professional teams now have interpreters who speak languages other than English. This provision is important for drawing foreign players, who in turn draw foreign fans. Foreign players come to their teams, showing appreciation and acceptance of this accommodation. Once management is able to display this level of understanding, employees begin to display greater job satisfaction and appreciation.

All employees must know the benefits of diversity. They should be able to see how a more diverse workforce will benefit them. When the number of customers increases, when the profit margin increases, or when the turnover rate decreases, share this information with your employees. Athletes begin to appreciate diversity when their playoff appearances increase or when their championship rings increase. Success has to be shared in order for employees to buy into diversity.

Acknowledging this success is the best way to increase diversity in the workplace. As mentioned before, many employees want to work in an environment that is comfortable. We are comfortable with familiar surroundings. Many of us do not want to disrupt that balance. Adding diversity to a stable group may seem like a mistake at first, but it actually works in favor of the group. There may be a great deal of resistance in the beginning, but if the goals are explained and the vision is shared, more employees will understand and most probably buy into diversity.

Implementing Diversity

When you are implementing diversity within your company, make the transition as smooth as possible. Don't put diversity under a magnifying glass and force it down everyone's collective throat. Instead, allow it to develop naturally. Being a part of a movement toward diversity can be highly challenging. The last thing a person who is already perceived as different needs is to be given more attention than desired. Encourage your staff to work together to create congruency and acceptance, without highlighting the differences.

Sylvester remembers a job interview he had a few years ago. At the time of the interview, he felt that some of the questions were strange and perhaps even inappropriate. He was asked about his acceptance of a particular group of people, and how he would feel working with them. When he was offered the position he realized why the interviewers had asked these questions. They were embracing diversity and wanted to be sure that Sylvester embraced it also.

While this company's effort to bring diversity to the organization was commendable, management had not informed the employees of the direction the company was taking. As a result, a stir was created within the organization and reactive damage control took place. Diversity in the workplace must be incorporated with employees' comprehensive awareness.

Embracing Diversity

Diversity, like variety, is the proverbial spice of life. Because one of the main goals of any business is growth, diversity is an important ingredient in an organization's repertoire. While the power of diversity in the workplace is clear, it is also obvious that companies don't always know how to fully embrace this concept.

First, the organization must have a desire to expand, because expansion will be the natural byproduct of a diversity initiative. Secondly, the company must understand that evolution is change. A company is ready for diversity when it is ready for growth and both the staff and management are willing to accept the evolution of the company.

When change occurs in our homes, we are more likely to be accepting if we are made aware of it beforehand. Sylvester was watching a popular sitcom a few weeks ago. In this episode, the male character had purchased a house without his wife's input. When he brought her to see the house, she absolutely adored it. She went from room to room just gushing over how beautiful the house was. When he told her that he was pleased she liked it because he had just purchased it, she became angry. She was disappointed that her husband hadn't consulted her on this major decision.

Diversity in a company becomes a welcomed change when the goals and objectives are discussed with your business "family" and the vision is shared. The employees understand the vision and can see how adding diversity will help achieve it. Diversity can be a scary concept but, when approached correctly, it can help the company grow and can increase the bottom line.

In the next chapter, we will outline some of the considerations to think about when hiring the diverse workforce you need.

Hiring the Diversity You Need

Many companies don't put a great deal of effort into creating a diverse workforce because it's scary. Diversifying the workforce means putting together a collection of individuals who are different and asking them to exist in a harmonious setting. The fact is, we are all naturally more comfortable in an environment where there are individuals with whom we can relate . . . who are more like us. We want to be able to walk into an office and feel that we know and understand (to some degree) the people with whom we are going to spend the next eight hours of our life.

When we come into the workplace, we want to feel as though we know the players and the informal rules. When this type of environment is created, employees feel a high level of comfort which translates into a more satisfied workforce. Everybody appreciates a homogeneous workplace because it is comfortable and pleasing. But how does this lack of diversity affect the bottom line?

Broadening your diversity base means broadening the opportunities to serve more customers more effectively. This not only increases your bottom line but it also makes your company more attractive to the customer. When customers feel that they are represented where they shop, they are more apt to be loyal.

In the field of social services, as well as education, most employees are female. The many young males who are in these systems do not often have an opportunity to connect with another male role model, because of the lack of gender diversity in these professions. There are mentoring programs that have young men on a waiting list to be matched with a male mentor. The problem is that there are very few male mentors to go around. The challenge becomes to attract more males to these professions.

This chapter offers suggestions to help you be more successful in your efforts to recruit for diversity.

Advertising

When advertising for a new position, you need to be clear within yourself about the qualities that you are seeking in a new employee. Where might you find individuals with these qualities? Post your job description in places where you know the applicants you want to hire frequent, such as job fairs in the communities and at the local colleges and universities. If you want to hire a Spanish-speaking applicant, then perhaps your ad should be written in Spanish and published in a newspaper bought in Spanish-speaking communities.

Think about what you know about the diversity you are trying to create. What would attract an applicant that you want? Is it possible to build that into the equation? In the social services example, is it possible that men are not attracted to that field because they are uncomfortable being supervised by a female?

This brings us to another point about representation. If you want to hire a minority, you better have some representation in your existing employees. It will be difficult to hire an African-American who only sees white faces when he is interviewing at your office. He may think that he will be the "token black" or that advancement isn't open to minority groups.

We did cultural awareness training for a company in Pennsylvania that was supervised by an openly gay lesbian. This woman supervised about 40 employees and was excellent at her job. During the training, it was revealed that approximately 60% of these 40 employees were gay. This is a very meaningful statistic when you consider that only 10% of the population is gay. Why would 60% be employed at this one company? The company wasn't serving gay clients; it was providing mental health services to adults. Nor did this woman hire all her gay friends. She had been transferred from another state and had simply gone about the business of staffing her branch. In doing so, she provided applicants with a role model of a known lesbian in a position of authority, and she offered an open and safe environment for gay employees to fully be themselves.

In addition to having minorities represented in your company, is your company represented in the community from which you are attempting to recruit? Many people like to work near their homes. Do you have offices or stores in the communities of the people you want to recruit? Trust is a huge issue with minority workers, as already discussed. Nothing builds trust faster than positive experiences. Recruiting workers from a community will be much easier if you have a presence in that community so that its members can get a sense of the work you do and the benefits it offers.

We also do training for a company in South Philadelphia that provides halfway house services for maximum security male parolees. The company's site is located in an area known to be dangerous. In fact, a taxi cab driver once refused to leave Kim in front of the building; he waited until he was certain that she had gotten safely inside. This program is run by a small-town Caucasian female who, on the surface, appears to have nothing in common with her clients or her diverse staff. How did she hire the staff? She had a consistent, positive presence in the community. Community members came to trust her as well as the work that was done in her facility.

So, how do you start recruiting a diverse workforce if all your current employees are white males?

Selling your company to prospective employees is important. Think of your company as a puzzle; your vision is the completed puzzle. When you know what the end product should look like, you have a clear understanding of what pieces belong in the puzzle. If you know what piece you need, you are less likely to force a piece into a place where it doesn't fit. The bigger the puzzle, the more pieces are needed to complete it. This may be challenging, but with patience, perseverance, and some trial and error, it can be done successfully.

So, sharing your vision with perspective employees is important. It gives them the opportunity to evaluate more effectively the possibility of working within your organization. When speaking with applicants, use words such as "diverse" and "varied" because these will send a clear message that you are thinking along broad hiring lines. Of course, this can be a fine line to walk because you can't hire a person simply based on race, gender, or ethnicity anymore than you can exclude someone from employment for these same reasons. However, you can write your ads in such a way that minorities will feel included and not discriminated against.

As previously mentioned, when you initiate a diversity program in the workplace, it is to your advantage to inform your present workforce of your intentions, your reasons, and the resulting benefits for both the company and the employees. As you refine your vision, keep employees informed of any changes or revisions. Inspire them by expressing your confidence that your vision will come to fruition. How can you expect your employees to get on board if they don't perceive your passion and dedication to the vision? Welcome their feedback, but understand that many of them are going to speak from a place of discomfort and fear of change. Remember, this is *your* vision and not everyone will see it as you do.

Interviewing

Interviews provide a rich opportunity for two-way communication. They set the tone for the job that follows. They offer the potential employees a glimpse into the strengths and the vision of the company.

Have your vision of diversity represented in the interviewing process. This will give the prospective employee a taste of your company and a more tangible experience with regard to your vision. Be sure that your interviewing questions are comprehensive. Obviously you want to use this time to find out all that you can regarding the interviewee; but this is also an opportunity for you to disclose aspects of your company, including your vision. For example, allowing yourself to share some of the company's vulnerabilities and areas of improvement will make you and your company more appealing. All employees involved in the interviewing process should spend time developing the questions based on the identified vision. This process will keep everyone focused and consistent within the process.

When setting up the interview, provide a variety of times that the prospect can come in. Time and availability are important to some cultures. Some are more available in the evenings while others are more available in the mornings. By providing a variety of scheduling opportunities, you are enhancing the possibility of attracting diverse cultures.

You also need to be cognizant of the environment in which you interview. Usually managers will interview in their office—a comfortable space for them, filled with creature comforts such as family pictures and other personal items. Although this may go unnoticed by the manager, the prospects are very much aware that they are in your domain and should conduct themselves accordingly. Try to make the environment where you hold the interview culturally sensitive and comfortable for them.

You may ask questions of interviewees regarding how they see themselves fitting into the productive, diverse workforce of your vision. What strengths do they bring to the table? Where do they place themselves on the continuum which ranges from strongly maintaining their personal, cultural identity to completely assimilating into the corporate culture? What, if anything, might they do if confronted with prejudice and discrimination in the workplace, involving themselves or someone else?

During interviews, you can find out what value your interviewees believe they bring to the company. You can also ask their opinions about how to create a more diverse workforce. What might they do if faced with this task? Asking for their suggestions in the interview will send the message that their opinions will be regularly sought and valued.

You can also ask interviewees to describe a past situation in which they were able to solve a problem creatively, or view a situation from a different angle than their managers. You may ask what challenges they believe minority groups face in the workplace and what solutions they have for fixing these problems.

Beware of Hiring for Minority Status Only

e.e.cummings said, "To like an individual because he is black is just as insulting as to dislike him because he is not white." We would add to this quote that it is equally as insulting to hire or promote employees based on the minority group to which they belong. We encourage you to value diversity, but not to value only the traits that make a person different. Diversity brings so much more to the table than heterogeneity! To hire someone just because he or she belongs to the "correct" group is just as damaging as the quota system in employment has been.

Benefits and Accommodations

The types of benefits offered to employees can have a large impact on the type of people who are attracted to the company. Some companies have health insurance plans that offer benefits to domestic partners. These will attract same-sex couples as well as committed co-habiting couples who are not married. Some companies provide a certain number of personal days off that employees can use for religious holidays and cultural celebrations. Still other companies provide a menu of benefits from which employees can choose.

Holidays and personal celebrations can be important to some cultures. Your ability to recognize and support them is critical to the camaraderie within your company. However, holidays can be tricky. Some of your employees may celebrate certain religious holidays not nationally recognized. Others may celebrate nationally recognized holidays that are not recognized by your company. Displaying a degree of sensitivity to these issues can be of great benefit to you, your employees, and your company.

When accommodating certain cultural issues, you may be walking a fine line. In an effort to accommodate certain requests, a manager may be discriminating against other employees. For example, if a mother is granted her request to start work later in the day so that she can get her children on the school bus, someone else may have to cover for her.

We believe that there are certain questions to ask yourself when considering accommodating a minority employee:

1. Would I be considering this request if a similar one were brought to me by a member of the majority culture?

2. Would honoring this request hurt the company in any way?

3. Would granting this request be unfair or cause hardship to another person or department?

If the answer to these questions is no, then ask yourself if the employees can work out the details themselves, if you provide a certain structure to the solution. For example, if a mother needs to come in late so that she can put her children on the bus, can you let her know that she is responsible for ensuring that there is coverage for her particular area during her absence?

Empowering Employees

As a manager, you should be clear to your employees about how much authority they have, and give them the responsibility for working out their own solutions. Not only does this empower employees, but it also frees you up to perform other tasks. However, it is important that you ask your employees to bring their solution to you for final approval, and only become involved in the details if they need your help.

This approach accomplishes several things:

First, you are not the "bad guy" anymore. The responsibility for fairness lies with the employees, as does the responsibility to reach a solution.

Secondly, you are consistently communicating the needs of the company to your employees in a way that makes sense and that they can understand. As the supervisor, you may have to monitor situations where you believe communication is not effective or an employee is being taken advantage of. Some employees may have been acculturated to be highly accommodating. You, as the supervisor, must monitor situations to ensure that a fair resolution is reached. You may want to investigate the situation personally, to ensure that the employee is really all right with the agreement reached.

Thirdly, your employees are offered ample opportunity to develop teamwork and group problem-solving skills.

And finally, your workers will gradually recognize the various values of diversity.

Orientation

When you bring new staff aboard, the first few days are crucial. Joining a company can be frightening to new employees, but you can ease some of that discomfort by helping them assimilate. You can make them aware of all of the formal strategies that have been put in place. You can introduce them to the other employees, so that they can begin to familiarize themselves with everyone. However, you should be careful not to make a spectacle of them.

A new employee's first day can be critical to his or her ability to appreciate diversity. To really embrace and encourage diversity, managers must make a conscious effort to recognize that there are differences and to encourage appreciation of these differences. Having cultural lunches and diversity discussions are just a couple of ways to encourage appreciation. Explain to the new employees why you have these lunches and sessions, and let them know that they are expected to take an active part in them.

These luncheons, in particular, are a great way to bring diverse cultures together. After making sure that employees are clear about what culture is, have employees bring to work a dish from their culture to share with everyone. Make sure that all employees are informed of the luncheon so that everyone feels represented. While having lunch, ask each employee to share why he or she brought that particular dish. You can have a topic prepared to discuss during these luncheons, or you can allow the group to simply share their food and have an informal conversation.

A diverse workforce will not only broaden opportunities to serve more customers, but it will also provide your employees with an opportunity to become more objective. When a company lacks diversity, it is likely that the employees will remain comfortable within their "familiar" surroundings and won't be open to embracing difference. You never know when diversity may be thrust upon you through a merger or a take over. Will your workforce be prepared for it?

The next chapter discusses how to retain the diversity that you have established.

Retaining the Diversity You Need

"We could learn a lot from crayons: some are sharp, some are pretty, some are dull, some have weird names, and all are different colors . . . but they all exist very nicely in the same box." —Unknown

All right, so now you've managed to hire a diverse workforce. You're done, right? Wrong! Hiring a diverse workforce is just the beginning. After that, comes the task of maintaining it.

Hiring diversity has been regulated by law since the 1960s, to provide everyone with equal employment opportunity. The risk to you, as the employer, for violating these laws is major litigation or a settlement out of court. As Dr. Sondra Thiederman writes in *Making Diversity Work*, "Discrimination suits are every executive's nightmare. This is, of course, no surprise when you look at figures like the $192 million, $157 million, and $176 million paid out by Coca-Cola, State Farm Insurance, and Texaco, respectively. Admittedly, most companies do not face damages as large as these, but even the more modest amount . . . combined with the hidden expense of attorneys' fees, employment practices, liability insurance, court costs, out-of-court settlements, and loss of reputation are enough to take the gloss off of anyone's annual report."[1]

"Over the last 10 years, according to data compiled by DiversityInc, major race- and gender-discrimination lawsuits cost U.S. corporations $974 million in settlements alone—and that's without attorney fees, decreased market capitalization and other costs."[2]

Dr. Thiederman then goes on to explain that the costs of discrimination to companies are threefold: diminished sales and accompanying lost customers, wasted time, and loss of employees. Dr. Thiederman reports that the costs associated with losing good employees can range from 25% of their annual salary up to 250% and beyond.[3] The first two costs will be discussed in the next chapter.

Now let's take a look at what workers are saying about diversity.

Employees' Perceptions, Problems, and Complaints

In the book, *Voices of Diversity: Real People Talk about Problems and Solutions in a Workplace Where Everyone Is Not Alike*, Renee Blank and Sandra Slipp interviewed many employees belonging to several different minority groups. What follows is a brief summary of these interviews, accompanied by our own observations and discoveries during our trainings.[4] *Although these problems are not true for every member of the selected groups, they serve as a general overview of some of the challenges you may face when attempting to retain diversity.*

Members of many cultures complain of being all lumped together under an umbrella minority culture that doesn't take their uniqueness into account. For example, the Asian-American and Latino groups include members from a variety of different cultures which prefer to be seen as distinct. Thus, Koreans are different from Japanese, just as Puerto Ricans are different from Mexicans. Gays and lesbians also speak about the diversity within their group that is often overlooked or even unknown to the heterosexual population.

Several cultural groups—such as African-Americans, Latinos, people with disabilities, and women—complain about the dominant culture's attitude towards them for taking jobs away from white males. They feel that white males resent them for their ambition and their desire to get ahead at work. Minorities also report that they are not viewed as individuals but rather as black, Hispanic, or disabled. It seems difficult for white males to accept laws that help women and minority groups because they perceive that these laws have negative consequences for them.

African-Americans believe that they cannot discuss racial issues with Caucasians because whites don't really believe that discrimination still exists. When blacks bring up incidents of inequity, whites often don't understand the situation or they think that the blacks are making a big deal out of nothing. They also think that blacks like to play the "race card" in order to get preferential treatment. African-Americans, on the other hand, believe that they have to be twice as good and work twice as hard as a white person, in order to get the same recognition for their accomplishments.

Furthermore, many minority employees feel the pressure of having to perform for their entire culture, as if they represent their entire group and the public perception of their group depends on their performance. When people feel that they are defined by their group and not their individuality, this idea of "global representation" is more likely.

Some groups complain that they are often asked intrusive questions: recent immigrants are often asked what was wrong in their country that prompted them to come here; disabled workers are asked intrusive questions about their disability; and homosexuals are often asked questions about their sexual lives.

A good rule of thumb for appropriate questions directed towards minorities is twofold:

- Ask yourself if you would like to be asked the question that you are about to ask.

- Ask yourself if you would ask a similar question of a person who belongs to the majority culture.

If the answer to either of these questions is no, then don't ask.

Entry-Level Positions

For many members of minority cultures, being hired for entry level positions is just the beginning. There are still roadblocks and uphill climbs.

African-Americans believe that they are often pigeonholed into support services or "black products" departments. They are not encouraged or permitted to take risks on the job.

Asian-Americans complain that they are stereotyped as being strong in the science, mathematics, and technical fields. As a result they are seriously considered only for such positions.

Latinos complain that they are frequently hired to work solely with a Spanish-speaking population, and aren't typically considered for working with mainstream clientele. They also believe that managers have low expectations of them on the job.

Workers with disabilities believe that they are frequently defined by their disability instead of being viewed as whole people capable of doing their job. They believe that they are rarely considered for promotions because employers already think they have gone to extraordinary measures just to hire them—and therefore disabled workers should be grateful to be employed at all.

Generational culture clashes are more prevalent now than ever before. Blank and Slipp learned that younger workers believe that information is withheld from them, and that they are excluded from job-related activities. For a more detailed discussion of culture along generational lines, please read *Generations at Work: Managing the Clash of Veterans, Boomers, Xers, and Nexters in Your Workplace* by Ron Zenke, Claire Raines, and Bob Filipczak.[5] Older workers complain that there is little or no flexibility on the job. Furthermore they believe that they are often encouraged to retire early or that they are forced out of their jobs.

Women are still making less money than their male counterparts. Pregnancy still creates discriminatory practices despite the Family and Medical Leave Act. Pregnant women may not be hired for a job due to pregnancy. If hired, they may be looked over for a promotion. When they return from maternity leave, they may have to learn new jobs because theirs is no longer available; this can be stressful despite the fact that the new job must have equal pay and equal benefits to the job left.

Fighting Stereotypes

Once on the job, those who are not a part of the mainstream corporate culture have to dispel stereotypes about their groups. However they will only be afforded the opportunity to do so if those from the dominant culture are willing to get to know them on an individual basis.

African-Americans are fighting the media's depiction of them as scary, criminal, and lazy.

Because Asian-Americans do not like conflict and public confrontation, they are often considered passive and obsequious, and consequently, taken advantage of in the workplace.

Latinos are stereotypically labeled as being poor, from low socio-economic status, and not respectful of the American business time sense.

Latinas and female Asian-Americans are often viewed as sex objects at work and are treated accordingly, sometimes resulting in sexual harassment situations.

Recent immigrants say that they are often treated as stupid, because their English isn't very good. Also, they are considered inferior because they elected to leave their country of origin.

People are often unsure how to behave with a disabled person. Workers with disabilities are often patronized, pitied, or treated like children, and are believed to be very dependent. Some people become impatient with them, not taking the time to understand the situation. Others are cautious about what they say around them, often speaking for or about them as if they were not there. Workers who have disabilities that can't be seen, AIDS for example, are reluctant to bring them up for fear of negative consequences.

Older workers are constantly fighting the stereotype that they are weak or in poor health. Younger workers often view them as workaholics, overly loyal to their managers and companies.

Gays and lesbians believe that their supervisors and co-workers are uncomfortable around them, avoiding conversations about sexual orientation. Many heterosexuals still believe that homosexuality is a lifestyle preference or personal choice. Some even act as if all homosexual males have HIV and can be contagious through casual workplace contact.

Women believe that men view them as emotional and, therefore, weak. During meetings, women are often assigned administrative tasks by men. Whenever a woman progresses in her career, many men attribute her success to her using her sexuality.

Even though society views white males as the ones in power in a company, oftentimes they feel powerless and vulnerable themselves; yet they are socialized not to show their vulnerability or lack of knowledge. White men, as members of the dominant culture, are afraid of saying anything that may be misinterpreted because they believe that others consider them to be sexist and racist.

Beware! Stereotypes lie in wait to be renewed at every turn. Anytime we encounter people who conform to our personal stereotypes, a flame is fanned and the stereotypes gain new life. A major current event can also fuel our prejudice. We spoke of these in previous chapters—critical events that polarize individuals along racial, sexual, religious, or other lines.

Culture Clashes

As previously discussed, diversity in the workplace can result in culture clashes and misunderstandings.

Asian-Americans don't like being interrupted—which frequently happens—viewing such behavior as rude.

Latinos are often confused by American's primary attention to tasks on the job. Their culture values relationships over tasks to be performed.

Recent immigrants think that their nonverbal behavior is often misunderstood in the workplace. They believe that others have no interest in understanding the nuances of their culture, simply expecting them to quickly assimilate.

Along generational lines, younger workers are not always deferential to authority; consequently, older workers say that they don't get the respect from younger workers that they are due.

While there have been great improvements in this area, many women still say that there is little flexibility in their work hours. As a result, it is difficult, if not impossible, for women to meet both their work requirements and family responsibilities. Sexual harassment continues to be an issue in the workplace, despite the laws to prevent it. Many women believe that they will be blamed if they report the offensive behavior. Part of the problem is that white males haven't really been taught how to work effectively with women. They frequently don't understand the subtle nuances of sexual harassment, and believe it only applies to unwelcome sexual advances.

Supervision, Mentoring, and Promotion

For a variety of reasons, members of minority cultures often do not get the same supervision, mentoring, and promotion opportunities as the majority corporate culture. Furthermore, minorities often think that they are overlooked for interdepartmental promotions so that their managers can continue to meet EEO (Equal Employment Opportunity) goals.

African-Americans believe that they either get no supervision on the job, or that their supervisors are overly critical of their work.

Asian-Americans believe that they are often held to a higher standard of work performance, but are rarely considered for promotions because they are viewed as too passive to lead.

Recent immigrants often complain that their managers are too aggressive.

Younger workers believe that they don't always get the feedback, training, and supervision necessary to improve their work performance. However, they are not always deferential to authority figures. Since they are coming on the scene with more specialized knowledge than many veterans on the job, younger workers don't believe that they need to put in a certain amount of time to be considered for promotion. They often complain that they are not taken seriously and don't get enough credit for what they do.

Older workers believe that younger workers are not comfortable supervising them. They also complain of not getting training in new trends and information, particularly in the technical field, possibly because managers believe in the old adage, "You can't teach an old dog new tricks."

Women believe they are excluded from the informal men's network—either directly or indirectly. They often feel ignored by men in meetings or during individual conversations and believe that men are not comfortable being supervised by them.

In general, minority groups and women believe that their road to promotion is hampered by not having appropriate mentors. People in higher positions tend to look for protégés who are similar to them. If employees don't look, act, and sound like those in higher positions, they will not get the one-on-one attention, grooming, and endorsement often necessary to be considered for promotion.

Many white men in senior positions are often discouraged from mentoring women because they fear sexual harassment accusations. They have difficulty giving negative feedback to women because they have been taught to be protective of them. They experience conflict about accommodating women on work/life balance issues because they want to be fair to everyone.

As was discussed in Chapter 13, in some professions, white males who befriend women or minorities on the job will be accused of compromising their culture.

Pressure to Conform

Once on the job, minorities often experience pressure—sometimes subtle and other times blatant—to conform to the culture of the corporate majority. After all, those with the power believe they've got it all figured out. They've been doing things the same way for years and that's worked just fine. Why change now?

When blacks achieve a management position, they report pressure to conform to white norms, which diminishes their pride in their racial origin and culture.

Latinos say they are pressured to conform to a more conservative standard of dressing, which is not in line with their taste or cultural norms.

Recent immigrants feel pressured to only speak English, even when working with others who speak their native tongue. Like Latinos, they too feel pressure to conform to mainstream standards for dressing.

Gays and lesbians often feel that they must hide their sexuality at work, in order to retain their credibility. Much of their energy is used in keeping this secrecy, thus affecting their ability to be productive. Homosexuals who are open about their sexuality say that they are often penalized for nonconformance with typical gender roles. There is no federal legal protection against discrimination based on sexual orientation. Heterosexuals are basically unaware of the discrimination that gays and lesbians experience in the workplace.

Women are expected to act like members of the majority culture (i.e. white men), by becoming aggressive and single-minded about work. They often need to relegate family matters to the background, in order to prove themselves equal to men. Many women see no room for advancement at their jobs and believe that they are passed over for promotion in favor of men—regardless of their qualities. Those women who do advance are often labeled negatively and are not liked by their peers.

White males often become frustrated with all the new information and skills necessary to effectively manage all the different groups that exist in the workplace.

Need for Connection

Minorities often feel criticized for wanting to spend time on the job with others who are like them. For example, African-Americans eating lunch together may meet with criticism from the majority culture that is attempting to integrate them. Latinos say they meet with resistance whenever they speak Spanish with their Spanish co-workers.

Recent immigrants complain that their spiritual beliefs, religious observances and holidays are not understood, and that few people attempt to understand their sense of grief about leaving their homeland.

There is one final thing to consider. In *Making Diversity Work*, Dr. Thiederman writes about a phrase she coined, Guerilla Bias™. She says, "Reasonable and respectful accommodation of cultural differences is, of course, a hallmark of a healthy diverse workplace . . . It is when managers fall into the trap of Guerilla Bias and bend over backward to accommodate any one group that trouble begins and productivity declines."[6]

She chose the phrase Guerilla Bias™ because this type of bias is often hidden, as in guerilla warfare. People using it are often unaware they are being biased and are simply trying to be nice.

A simple way to check on your possible Guerilla Bias™ is to ask yourself if you believe a certain target group requires special and preferential treatment because they are somehow fragile and in need of protection. Are you concerned about hurting someone's feelings, getting someone upset or offended? If yes, then you are most likely in the area of Guerilla Bias™.

Steps to Take to Aid Retention

Managers must take whatever steps are necessary to combat the complaints listed above. Here are some steps we believe will help:

1. Workers need to understand the company's mission, vision, and values, as well as their role within the company.

2. Managers must create a corporate culture that communicates that differences are not only tolerated—they are welcomed. Everyone has value; every perspective has merit. Everyone must relinquish the idea that there is only one way to do things. The thought that one person is doing something "wrong" must be substituted with the word "different."

3. A leader's job is to define the outcome of a particular task or project, allowing the workers to determine the way it will be accomplished.

4. Workers need to function in an environment where their five basic human needs can be met, as defined by Dr. William Glasser in *The Control Theory Manager*:[7]

   a. ***Survival*** refers to a person's need to not only have their physiological needs met, but also to feel safe and secure. On the job, this means that employees need to be free of the fear that their job is in jeopardy and free from the negative consequences of prejudice. This can be accomplished by asking all employees to be on the lookout for any inequity in the workplace, and providing a forum to report such inequities so that they can be investigated. Minority workers will feel much safer if there are specific allies from the dominant culture identified to help them report the inequities to the appropriate people.

b. ***Love & Belonging*** is the need people have to be accepted and liked by others who are important to them. For most people, having their co-workers' and manager's approval is important. Ways to accomplish this would be to have open forum discussions on a regular basis, facilitated by skilled individuals, regarding diversity issues. Seek out ways to recognize and represent the cultures that are a part of your workforce. Create opportunities for team building experiences. Create social opportunities for people. Pair minority workers with receptive individuals from the dominant culture for mentoring and social inclusion.

c. ***Power*** refers to the need people have to feel important, recognized, and respected. At work this translates into being valued. You can ask employees' opinions regarding how to accomplish certain goals and give each suggestion equal consideration. You can evaluate whether accommodations for cultural, generational, or gender issues can be made without affecting the overall performance of the team. Consistently send the message that individuals do not need to conform to a cookie cutter mold of corporate culture in order to be considered for promotion. Allow individuals to retain as much of their culture as possible without penalty.

d. ***Freedom*** refers to the need people have to do things their own way—to do what they want, when they want. Obviously, business owners cannot give their workers carte blanche to do anything they want; there would be utter chaos. But at work, providing freedom often translates into allowing individuals the space to carry out their job functions without micromanagement by supervisors. In the case of minorities, however, managers should be careful. Often minorities are left to do things their own way without receiving the necessary feedback to help them improve their performance. This may meet their need for freedom while frustrating their need for power. How can they improve their performance if they are unable to get adequate feedback from their managers?

e. ***Fun*** is the final need, which seems self-explanatory. People need to enjoy what they do. This is most aptly described in Stephen Lundin, Harry Paul, and John Christensen's book, *Fish!: A Remarkable Way to Boost Morale and Improve Results.*[8] It tells the story of a Seattle-based fish market called Pike Place Fish where employees love to come to work because they experience fun on the job everyday. Glasser's other component of fun is what he calls the genetic reward for learning. He tells us that learning useful information that we can apply to our lives is fun. This is something that can be implemented at work—training, coaching, or mentoring programs that help move employees to the next level in their careers.

We believe that all companies can establish diversity, but the true test comes in maintaining it. By understanding some of the concerns that different groups share, and by developing and following a strategic plan, you will enhance your chances of retaining your diverse workforce.

In Chapter 19 we will discuss ways to inspire and leverage your diverse workforce.

Inspiring and Leveraging Diversity

"We may have come over on different ships,
but we're all in the same boat now."
–Whitney Young, Jr.

Once you have managed to obtain diversity within your organization, you must inspire employees to maintain it. Having a workforce that is inspired to preserve your vision of diversity is refreshing and encouraging. As parents, we often have similar desires for our children. We want them to embrace our values and morals. When they begin to demonstrate a genuine grasp of our values, we feel very proud. As a business manager, you can experience this same feeling with your employees.

Employees must feel that everyone is very important to the success of the company. When they feel that diversity is critical and necessary, they will have a more objective, non-judgmental attitude which will create an atmosphere of togetherness and oneness in the work place. This is one of the most significant stages to business growth.

There are several areas that you can focus on to increase your chances of securing an inspired workforce.

Professional Development

When we do trainings, we are passionate about the information we provide because we strongly believe in it. As passionate as we are, we fully realize that change does not happen overnight. None of this is *easy!* Therefore, professional development is necessary. Your employees must be given the opportunity to grow as individuals, as well as professionals. You may assemble the most diverse workforce ever known to man, but without professional development, you will not be able to inspire diversity.

As previously discussed, we cannot learn about a different culture by reading a book. We first need to know members of that culture personally. Once we've had the opportunity to know them, we need information so that we can understand the barriers that are preventing us from embracing their culture. Professional development provides this information. The more your employees are exposed to information regarding diversity, the more likely they are to want to maintain a diverse workforce.

Professional development is critical because it allows employees to receive your message from a third party. Have you ever provided information to a person who just didn't seem to get it? Your employees are more likely to accept your vision and goals through a third party. Furthermore, they will have the opportunity to ask questions or make comments in an environment that they may perceive as safe and non-threatening.

Some companies are investing in professional coaches for high level managers to help them accomplish their goals. Professional coaches provide support through difficult times and hold managers accountable for the goals they set. Coaches can also assist employees to transfer learning from the training room to the job. During training, many employees are inspired to change their behavior but often, when they get back to the job, they are unable to implement these changes. People tend to continue doing things the way they always have. A coach can help break this pattern.

Proper Integration

Were you ever given a task where you just didn't know what you were doing? Having a responsibility that you feel totally incapable of meeting is very frightening. New employees often feel this way. The excitement of a new job can quickly turn into frustration, or even fear, without the proper integration strategy. Seasoned employees can assist new employees in adapting to the company and should be included in the welcoming and orientation of newly hired or transferred employees.

Setting up shadowing or mentoring programs offers veteran employees the opportunity to take an active part in the grooming of new hires. This gives seasoned employees a stronger sense of ownership in the company. One signal that the level of ownership is increasing among employees is when they use the term "we" instead of "they" when discussing the company. This change in the employees' language is a true indicator that they have bought into the company's vision and are inspired to maintain diversity.

You, as a manager, have the opportunity to encourage this kind of behavior. When your employees hear you speaking in a way that is inclusive, they feel that they matter and they become more invested in the company. This results in a feeling of security and safety in the workplace.

Events

Special events can be used to inspire staff. Employees love the opportunity to meet in a way that is less formal and more fun. Whenever you can bring a smile or a feeling of joy to your employees, you have created an environment that they are drawn to and one that they will want to maintain and continue to be a part of. You've heard the saying, "All work and no play makes Jack a dull boy." All work may increase production, but it won't do much to inspire your staff.

Developing a system where birthdays or hiring anniversaries are formally recognized is always a good idea. (However, keep in mind that there are some cultures, particularly certain religious groups, that do not celebrate birthdays.) Events such as company picnics and holiday celebrations are also popular. Many companies have promoted sporting events as events to be shared by all. These events can include family, thus providing the opportunity for even more diversity. Anytime you can provide employees with an opportunity to relieve some stress, relax, and just be themselves, you are increasing the likelihood that they will work towards maintaining the organization's environment.

Another way is to recognize and honor dates of importance for your diverse workforce. Go to www.coachingforexcellence.biz/calreg.htm to download your diversity calendar, with many multicultural events, celebrations, and historical moments. This is our free gift to you to enhance what you already do for your employees.

Establishing a Satisfying Environment

Picture this. You are alone on an elevator, going up to the 25th floor. As the elevator moves you begin to feel comfortable; you may even begin to sing a little song. Your body starts relaxing and you are feeling very content. Then the elevator stops, the door opens and in walk two strangers. How do you feel now? The simple, unexpected addition of two people in the elevator can completely change the environment from relaxed to tense. Environment is important.

We are constantly seeking to establish comfort. When we are in a room and the temperature is too cold, we might put on an extra layer to be more comfortable. Barbara Jordan (the first black woman from the South to serve in the U.S. congress) once said, "How do we create a harmonious society out of so many kinds of people? The key is tolerance, the one value that is indispensable in creating community." We prefer to use the word "acceptance" instead of "tolerance." After all, who wants to merely be tolerated? When we are more accepting of others, we create an environment that is very satisfying.

The physical environment of the workplace is important. Everything from the accessories in the restroom to the pictures on the walls can affect the comfort level of an employee. Ambiance is a highly underrated aspect of the work environment. An employee who feels a sense of peace and calm when working is more likely to be effective and inspired to work harder.

The internal environment is even more important than the physical environment. By internal environment, we mean programs and strategies to help employees with issues that might affect how they perform at work. Helping employees establish and maintain a good attitude is essential. This also goes back to letting them know that you care about them and that you have their well-being in mind.

Some employees may have relationship problems which are affecting not only their performance, but even their ability to come to work. If they are afforded some sort of assistance while at work, they are more likely to show up. The kind of programs offered must be conducive to assisting *all* employees regardless of race, gender, religion, age, physical ability, or sexual orientation. This kind of comprehensive approach will encourage all of your employees to look to you and the company in their time of need.

Useful Meetings

One of the most frustrating issues for employees is being asked to attend a meeting that they find meaningless and useless. Companies often have large meetings, inviting many employees who don't see the purpose of the meeting and who don't benefit from it. Furthermore, many meetings go on for hours, with much of that time spent discussing issues that many employees find useless. Meetings are useful when all employees involved see the benefit of the meeting and have a vested interest in it. When issues that concern the employees are addressed, their interest goes up and they are inspired.

Employees are more apt to attend meetings when they feel that the time spent is beneficial. In football games, generally before each play, there is a huddle. In this huddle, a particular play is called and each member of the team is given a responsibility. Similarly, all attendees of a meeting should feel that they are important and that their role is crucial to the team's success. As a manager, you need to reiterate to employees the importance of their responsibility to the success of the company.

One of the methods used to enhance the possibility of having more meaningful meetings is a suggestion box. Suggestion boxes give employees the opportunity to address issues that are relevant to them—anonymously. Suggestion boxes inspire input and inclusion in a non-intrusive way.

Another way to make meetings more productive is to distribute an agenda prior to the meeting so that attendees know the purpose of the meeting and what their role in it is. Time should be spent on each item as allocated, moving on to the next item when the time is up. Managers can follow up individually with any employee who didn't have enough time to provide all the information needed.

Benefits and Motivation

Benefit packages, while important to all companies, are particularly important in a company that embraces diversity. Benefits need to go beyond the basics, discussed in Chapter 18. There are other benefits you can offer employees that will inspire them: financial planning seminars, annual health screenings, on-site childcare, and tuition reimbursement, to name a few. Such perks serve to motivate employees to do a good job.

Keeping your staff motivated is important. A highly motivated staff is a staff with high morale. However, keeping your finger on the pulse of the morale within your company can be difficult. Employees often feel that they can't trust managers, which is why working to establish quality relationships is so important. When your employees know that you are genuinely concerned about them, they will welcome you into the fold and you will be able to gauge their morale.

People are motivated when they feel that they are being heard and that they are making a difference. Encouraging innovation and potential will also keep your staff motivated. Motivation is a feeling of being stimulated. In order to stimulate your staff, you must know what they value and then provide it as much and as often as possible.

Because your employees will come from various cultural backgrounds, they will have different ways of dealing with emotional setbacks. Your job is to identify various ways to motivate them so that they will stay inspired to do a good job. A highly motivated staff will have less turnover and better production. Low turnover will result in your staff being comfortable, familiar, and committed to the success of the company.

Supporting your employees' ideas motivates them to continue to think about new ways to improve the company. Encourage them to stretch themselves to reach higher heights. Encourage your employees to evaluate where they are in the company. Have them gauge their level of satisfaction and develop a plan of action to increase it. Many employees get bogged down in dissatisfaction and do not allow themselves to think of alternative ways to deal with challenging situations. Encouraging your employees to constantly self-evaluate will help them create and control change where it matters most . . . within. As your company grows and new employees are hired, the process of breaking them in will be easier because they will be influenced by a highly motivated, seasoned staff.

Inspiring your staff to maintain diversity is tantamount to increasing the company's level of success. However, inspiration will not happen overnight and is not something that you, as a manager, can do alone. Inspiring employees requires effort and takes time and patience. Don't get discouraged if it doesn't occur soon. Inspiring diversity will come, as long as the staff truly understands and sees the value of diversity in the workplace. Once this understanding takes place, leveraging diversity is right around the corner.

Leveraging Diversity at Work

Companies that invest the time, energy, and resources to create a diverse workforce can expect to reap many benefits. In the last chapter, we mentioned how Dr. Thiederman discussed three ways that discrimination costs companies: in diminished sales and lost customers, in wasted time, and in loss of employees.[1] We mentioned that the cost of employee turnover can be astronomical; thus, employee retention becomes a big factor in increasing a company's profit.

DiversityInc collects data from their "Top 10 Companies for Recruitment & Retention" and found the retention rates for those companies are "extremely high—between 91 percent and 94 percent—for everyone: whites, blacks, Asian Americans, Latinos and women. This shows they are connecting with all of their employees and, therefore, their customers, investors and suppliers as well."[2]

Diversity can be leveraged in terms of increased sales and increased customers. When companies fail to have a workforce that represents the clientele it serves, the clientele will leave. As stated previously, people like to do business with others who are like them. In the past, this hasn't always been possible. But now you can be one of those cutting edge companies that hires a diverse workforce, making it easier for clients and customers to spend their money where they feel comfortable.

"Take time to assess the individual needs of your customer" is Dr. Thiederman's commonsense advice.[3] This is difficult to accomplish when you have no one on staff that represents your customer base. Even though it is possible to develop empathy for other cultures, people can only think from their own cultural perspective. They only see the world through their cultural lenses. Having someone on staff from the group you wish to market to or serve will help increase your sales because the perspectives will match.

So how can you leverage your time when managing a diverse workforce? Won't you have to spend more time trying to manage employees with all these cultural differences? We don't want to mislead you into thinking that you will have an immediate payoff of time leverage. You will have to invest a great deal of time initially for staff development, individual coaching, considering special accommodations and requests, and mediating disputes.

However, time will become your friend when you make a firm commitment to hire, retain, and inspire the diverse workforce you need. As your employees understand their role in making diversity work, there will be fewer disputes. They will learn how to work out their own accommodations with each other. There will be a decreased need for training and coaching. Employees will adjust to the change and relinquish their self-centered bouts of intolerance, or they will find another place to work.

Teams will function better. More creative ideas will be generated. Solutions will be considered from multiple angles. When you become a pioneer in leveraging diversity, other companies will look to you and your accomplishments. They will want to know how you've created the harmonious, diverse workforce that you have. You will become an expert and forerunner in the field, mentoring other companies, which will increase your bottom line.

Leveraging diversity is the ultimate payoff. Many people have dreams of having the finer things in life; with discipline and focus, they can obtain them. They can have that car they desire. They can purchase that beautiful home. However, having the knowledge and the ability to maintain them is key.

Although leveraging diversity is a goal that all companies should strive for, the fact is that this process requires a great deal of effort. Many managers are not completely committed to investing the time, energy, and resources required to reach that level. When you can establish a workforce that embraces difference, you will see the payoff in terms of employees who deliver peak performance and increased profits for your company.

In our final chapter, we will discuss the steps necessary in making the commitment to hire, retain, and leverage a diverse workforce.

Making the Commitment

"Diversity without unity makes about as much sense as dishing up flour, sugar, water, eggs, shortening and baking powder on a plate and calling it a cake."
                                                    —C. William Pollard

Moving beyond the inequities that exist in most companies today will not be easy. You have been asked to scrutinize your company to identify some of the informal systems that probably exist, which separate employees who are different. Since this is a never-ending process rather than a destination, it will take time. It is fair to say that hiring, retaining, and inspiring your diverse workforce will probably take several years—so prepare yourself for the long haul.

Remember, the journey of a thousand miles begins with the first step—so why not get started today? The United States is made up of many cultures; the sooner your company capitalizes on this diversity, the better!

If you look around your company and see no disharmony, this could mean one of three things:

- There is no disharmony.

- Some disharmony exists just below the surface, waiting for a pivotal event to bring it to the surface.

- Employees are afraid to speak about the injustices because they fear there will be serious repercussions if they do. In this situation as the CEO or a member of the management team, you will probably not be told the truth.

Groups that historically have experienced injustice, prejudice, and oppression have major trust issues. They don't trust people in positions of authority; they don't trust members of the majority culture; and they don't trust any minority who is reaping some benefit from the majority culture. Therefore, if you have a black man on your board of directors, don't assume that minority workers will trust him just because his skin is the same color as theirs. If he is a member of *your* board, then your employees' perception may be that he will be unwilling to stand up for minority workers because doing so could jeopardize his tenuous position of power.

Trust is a major variable, built through the establishment of quality relationships. While having gender or race in common can create a sense of comfort, it does not necessarily create trust.

Cultural Diversity Continuum

The *PA Child Welfare Competency-Based Training and Certification Program* teaches the cultural diversity continuum with its six general positions.[1] Let's see where your company falls on the cultural diversity continuum. For an accurate assessment, you will most likely require the assistance of an outside, unbiased consultant, who can offer an assurance of confidentiality.

At the bottom of the continuum lies **cultural destructiveness**. At this low end, the company has attitudes, policies, and practices that are destructive to minority cultures and to the individuals within them. Oppression and discrimination are actively practiced, possibly with a certain approval from upper management. At the very least, management ignores these offenses.

The next step up is called **cultural incapacity**. At this level, a company is not intentionally destructive to minority cultures, but it lacks the capacity or the willingness to assist minorities. Its system remains extremely biased. The dominant culture believes in its own superiority and discriminates in its hiring and promotion of minorities. Segregation is promoted and stereotypes are perpetuated. Resources are allocated discriminately. Certain minority members may receive some small privileges, based upon their ability to assimilate or to know their place.

At the center of the continuum, lies *cultural blindness*. At this level, employees believe that culture and skin color simply don't matter. They believe that the policies and procedures of the dominant culture fit everyone in the company—that there is full-scale applicability. Cultural strengths are not recognized. The majority group considers minorities to be culturally deprived, and encourages them to assimilate. Those who don't assimilate are isolated.

The fourth position on the continuum is called *cultural pre-competence*. At this level the company recognizes that improvements can be made to some of their policies and procedures. However, it often believes that the small efforts made have a larger impact than they really do. The company does not go beyond its initial efforts, often lacking information on how to proceed.

The next position is termed *cultural competence*. At this level, the company accepts and respects differences, engaging in a continuous self-assessment of where it is in terms of diversity. It actively expands cultural knowledge and resources. The needs of the consumer and the dynamics of differences are priorities. The company commits to policies that enhance the products and services to diverse consumer groups and actually seeks advice and consultation from members of non-dominant cultures.

At the pinnacle of the continuum, lies the category of *cultural proficiency*. In this position, the company respects all cultures and seeks to add to its knowledge base. The organization advocates for cultural competence throughout its system.

To what level is your company committed? Is cultural pre-competence enough for you? Or do you really want to place your company on the cutting edge by committing to achieving cultural proficiency?

Outlined below are the steps necessary to move higher along the cultural diversity continuum.

Self-Assessment

Because the most effective changes in business occur from the top down, it is important for you, as the CEO or upper management, to ask yourself some difficult questions:

1. How much of your personal/social time is spent with people who are culturally different than you?

2. When you do spend time with culturally different people, do you spend that time openly learning about their culture or do you assert your own cultural preferences?

3. Do individuals of another culture represent *all* members of their culture to you? Or do you get to know them personally, learning more about their own experiences?

4. How comfortable are you when you are the only one of your culture in a culturally different group?

5. At work, how much time do you spend in cross-cultural exchanges with colleagues? When you do, do you discuss superficial issues, or do you risk engaging in serious conversation that could expose your lack of knowledge and possibly your fears?

6. Other than the occasional workshop, how much have you actually done to improve your knowledge and understanding of culturally different groups?

7. What personal and professional sacrifices are you willing to

make now for the long-term benefit of leveraging the diversity of your workforce?

8. How much risk have you taken by approaching your colleagues with the goal of bridging cultural differences within your workforce?

9. If you have presented yourself as being an expert in the area of cultural diversity—but you are not—are you willing to stop?

10. Are you willing to commit the necessary time and resources to move your company to a place where all employees are treated fairly—where their differences are sought out, celebrated, and valued?

If, in your self-assessment, you discover areas where you can improve, then get started! Move out of your comfort zone and allow your employees to see you as vulnerable. You will gain their respect and commitment that way—more so than simply sitting behind your desk and telling them what you think they should do. Remember, a diversity talk is no substitute for a diversity walk.

Key Personality Characteristics

According to William Sonnenschein in *The Diversity Toolkit: How You Can Build and Benefit from a Diverse Workforce*, managers need seven key personality characteristics to model good diversity management skills[2]:

1. Respect
2. Tolerance
3. Flexibility
4. Self-Awareness
5. Empathy
6. Patience
7. Humor

How do you measure up?

Vision

You must openly and repeatedly share your vision of diversity with your managers and ultimately with your entire workforce. All your employees should be able to reiterate the direction that you are leading your company, as well as their integral part in the new initiative. People are more comfortable on a journey when they know where they are going. Employees can make an informed decision about whether they want to stay on your bus which is headed in the identified direction, or whether they want to exit your bus and get on someone else's or start driving their own.

Create a shared mission with all employees which is in harmony with your vision of cultural diversity. Allow their input. Explore the values of your employees, finding common values along which to connect. There are some universal principles that seem to cut across cultures which Stephen Covey discusses in *The 8th Habit*: "fairness, kindness, respect, honesty, integrity, service, and contribution," to name a few.[3] Find values that everyone can agree on, to create a common direction and point of agreement.

Is Your Company Ready?

If your company is to move ahead with a diversity initiative, your employees must have the courage to identify and confront their own personal resistance, anger, and most importantly, fear. While this is a monumental task, it is definitely possible and certainly well worth the effort. You can encourage your employees to constantly ask themselves: "Is what I'm doing or thinking, effectively moving me toward the desired vision?"

This phase will most likely require some outside consultation. You are asking your employees to do some challenging introspection and, possibly, to change much of what feels right to them as part of their culture. Adjusting their culture and beliefs is very difficult. They have spent their lives trusting and believing what they've learned from their culture. Making the shift will require an objective, trusted voice. Hiring a consultant to assist in this process will be highly beneficial.

Once members of your majority culture understand the value of diversity—not simply because it is the just and fair thing to do, but also because it will enhance the overall work experience and improve the company's bottom line—then they must commit to becoming allies for those employees who have lacked power in your company: women, blacks, Asians, Hispanics, Jews, Muslims, gays, or others.

Listed below are standards of behavior for employees from the majority culture, as well as minority employees. If you are serious about effectively managing diversity at your company, you must let all employees know that these new job competencies are highly valued by the company. Let them know these competencies will be assessed during their regular supervision and will be included in their overall evaluations.

Standards of Behavior for the Majority Culture

As a leader, you want to be sure that you yourself are an ally to the minority employees in your company and you want your employees to be allies. We are asking members of the majority corporate culture to become advocates of those without corporate power by committing to the following standards of behavior:

1. *Understand that racism, sexism, ageism, and other "isms" are everywhere.* Just because people don't actively engage in discrimination doesn't mean that they are not a part of the bigger institutionalized racist, sexist, ageist system that perpetuates prejudice and oppression.

2. *Listen openly.* People won't tell their story if they think that others aren't interested. Even worse, if they believe that there will be negative consequences for making a complaint, they will remain silent. Members of the majority culture must honestly present themselves as safe people, who listen to the opinions of those who believe they have been treated unfairly. While some minorities may hold beliefs of injustice that are inaccurate, their feelings need to be valued and respected.

3. *Learn about yourself and your heritage.* Understand yourself first by actively pursuing a process of self-education. Assess your attitudes and behaviors, as they contribute to or combat prejudice. Reevaluate your language, to determine if you use terms or phrases which may be offensive to others, and discontinue their use. Again, this process does not happen overnight; but just the fact that you are becoming aware of these offenses is positive.

4. *Leave your comfort zone* and make friends with people who are different. Seek out the commonalities and connect on that level.

5. *Give up denial.* Be willing to examine and relinquish privilege when it is afforded to you simply because of your membership in the dominant culture. This will be particularly difficult if it means giving up some personal advantage for the greater good of the whole; but it needs to happen to create a true spirit of diversity within the company.

6. *Work together with others.* This means more than grudgingly working side by side with those who look, act, and think differently than you. It means having a true sense of teamwork, and understanding the value that each individual member brings to the overall success of the group.

7. *Educate others.* Marcus Gentry says, "The more you know, the more you owe."[4] It is your duty and obligation to share what you know in the area of diversity. Do not educate yourself only to keep what you know secret. Others can benefit from your research, wisdom, and experience. Also, take steps to implement discussions or workshops designed to promote understanding of racism and other "isms", to unite people.

8. *Risk discomfort.* Taking a stand against unfair practices, prejudice, and oppression is risky, particularly when you are a member of the majority group. It may be difficult for a heterosexual to take a stand against homosexual oppression

because of the fear of being perceived as a homosexual one-self. Risk bringing upon yourself the very behavior against which you are fighting.

9. *Take a public stand against injustice.* Speak loudly. Interrupt prejudice and take action against oppression. As Edmond Burke said, "All that is necessary for the triumph of evil is that good men do nothing."[5] You may not change the world, but you can affect individuals within it.

10. *Maintain a clear and strong vision of the end result*—a multicultural company that is dedicated to creating a quality workplace for everyone and to offering the best possible products and services—made possible by the multicultural approach to problem solving, marketing, and product development.

Standards of Behavior for Minorities

As a minority working in an environment where diversity is being encouraged, there are several things that you can do to make the transition smoother. There are some who would think we are blaming the victim but it is our intention to empower those who have been oppressed to understand that there are some things that they can do to make their situation better:

1. *Understand that privilege just is.* Do not take it personally. Members of the majority culture are not consciously operating under the belief that they have privilege.

2. *Be aware that if you look for injustice, you will find it.* Because of years and years of oppression and mistreatment, many minorities may encourage an environment that breeds mistreatment by looking for things that are not there.

3. *Know who you are.* Spend time understanding who you are and evaluating why you see and perceive things the way you do. Decide who you want to be and develop behaviors to get there.

4.   *Prepare to work harder* and more diligently than the majority culture. Yes, there is privilege in the world. Know that you may have to work harder than someone in the majority culture. Don't fight it. Just do it!

5.   *Learn to trust the majority culture.* Frank Crane said, "You may be deceived if you trust too much, but you will live in torment if you don't trust enough!"[6] Besides, you have probably been deceived more by people who are like you than those who are different.

6.   *Recognize and admit your own "isms."* Minorities also have prejudices which, if not recognized, can cloud their ability to be objective.

7.   *Don't make excuses.* Your culture is your culture. Work to overcome stereotypes by stretching yourself. It is not easy and you may suffer some backlash, but don't be denied! Anything worth having is worth fighting for.

8.   *Don't limit yourself.* Trying new things and incorporating new behaviors can be uncomfortable, but comfort is not always the best thing! The more you push your comfort zone, the better you will adjust to new situations and environments.

9.   *Don't feel that you are betraying your culture.* When you embrace diversity, others may see you as a "sell out." But as long as you remain true to yourself and you know who you are, you have no reason to avoid diversity.

10. *Never give up!* There will be times when your efforts may seem futile. This process may take years and there will be disappointments along the way. Just hang in there and stay committed to growing and embracing diversity.

Additional Steps for Creating Harmonious Multicultural Experiences

Staff development and coaching are critical elements in a diversity initiative. The first phase of staff development involves cultural awareness training for all employees. This is an experiential training designed to help both minorities and those with the power to develop a better understanding of each other's position, thoughts, and feelings.

Following that, it is imperative to have training in the area of cultural information. This training provides employees with information regarding certain cultural trends and tendencies. Please note that while cultural information provides some point of reference when working with someone from another culture, it is not meant to be conclusive or to replace personal experience.

Training in the area of cultural skills is also necessary. This provides employees with practical situations to develop the necessary skills to communicate cross-culturally.

Our recommendation is that you have someone outside your company come in to do these trainings. Diversity training requires specialized skills in the facilitation of differences. Just because someone is from a minority group does not qualify him or her to be a diversity trainer. Make sure you bring in a professional to train your employees in diversity.

Finally, offer coaching services, particularly to your managers. A coach can help employees transfer to their jobs what they've learned from staff development training. Eventually, you will be able to use your own employees as coaches. Naturally, some employees will be more skilled in the area of diversity than others. If they have a passion for doing this type of work, they can serve as coaches to employees who are having trouble implementing the diversity initiative.

Examine All Systems and Policies

Go back over all your policies and procedures, seeking out bias and inequity. Scrutinize them for any evidence of favoritism towards one group over another. Whenever you find inequity, change it. Be willing to confront and isolate culturally insensitive behavior. Advocate for those who are experiencing unjust behavior. Work things out in an atmosphere of safety, cooperativeness, and mutual respect. Always seek input from your employees in an attempt to create equity for all. As a manager, agree on the goal or task you want accomplished, but allow your team to work out the details on how it will be done.

Examine your hiring practices, your benefit package, and the accommodations you are willing or unwilling to make. Examine your staff development and mentoring programs. Are they working to support diversity? If not, revamp them.

Finally, communication is crucial. Have employees who are involved in cultural conflict admit their fears, discomfort, and uncertainty. Each person involved in the conflict should admit his or her part. Allow one person to talk at a time. The people talking should maintain the floor until they feel that the other parties understand their viewpoint. Others are allowed to ask them clarifying questions and offer empathic responses; but they are not allowed to communicate how they feel until the person talking admits feeling understood by everyone involved. Then, the next person gets his or her turn to speak, until everyone has had the opportunity to be heard and understood.

Some ground rules to consider:

- Avoid absolutes such as "always" and "never."

- Avoid categorizations that label people based on their membership to a particular group, such as: "Why can't you *men* ever say how you feel?" or "How come you *women* always have to be so emotional?"

- When communicating, use I-statements to take personal ownership of your own thoughts and feelings.

- Don't try to speak for other people.

- Do not use the second person "you," which creates an accusatory atmosphere.

If you have completed this book, congratulations! This means you have just taken the first step to create significant changes in your company that will really boost morale and propel you ahead of your competition in the 21st Century. Don't stop now. Keep your momentum moving. Make a commitment today to establish cultural diversity in your company. Call Coaching for Excellence, LLC today at 1-866-391-3034 for your free, no-strings-attached, 30-minute consultation.

Final Thoughts

"This is not the end. It is not even the beginning of the end.
It is, perhaps, the end of the beginning."
—Winston Churchill

Congratulations! You completed the first step of reading this book. *Leveraging Diversity at Work* is no easy task, as you've probably gathered. It can be challenging, intelligent and incredibly rewarding.

You have probably taken mental inventory of your company's strengths and areas for improvement in the area of diversity. Most likely, there are many things you are already doing to hire, retain and inspire your diverse workforce but you may be wondering where you go from here.

Please don't miss this call to action. If you don't take the necessary steps to leverage the diversity in your company, you will quickly be surpassed by those who are. Demographics are clear. Estimates project that by the year 2050, whites will be the numerical minority in the United States. Couple that with the fact that baby boomers are retiring at an alarming rate without enough younger workers to replace them, and that makes a strong case for forward thinking companies to embrace diversity.

If there is anything we can do to help you in your forward movement, please don't hesitate to ask. Go to www.coachingforexcellence.biz and sign up for our free ezine, delivered monthly to your email inbox. Check out our free chat page where you can log on at the weekly designated time and chat with one or both of us about issues that you are facing. And don't forget to download your **FREE Diversity Calendar** (see p. 174).

We are available to provide diversity training to your workforce and/or personal or group coaching to your company's leaders and managers.

As a person who purchased our book, *Leveraging Diversity at* Work, you are entitled to a free 30-minute consultation, no strings attached. Simply contact us at 1-866-391-3034 to schedule your consultation time. Let us know how we can better serve you.

With Deep Appreciation,

Kim Olver   Sylvester Baugh

Notes

Introduction

1. Allen, A. A. "Learning to Give: Quotes by Adela Allen." http://learningtogive.org/search/quotes/Display_Quotes. asp?author_id=714&search_type=author

Chapter 1

1. Hall, E.T. (1976). *Beyond Culture* (p. 16). Garden City, NY: Anchor Press/Doubleday.

2. *Nelson Study Bible* (Rev. standard version). (1952). Camden, NJ: Thomas Nelson Inc. Matthew 5:39.

3. *Nelson Study Bible* Matthew 5:38.

4. Covey, Stephen, R. (1989). *The 7 Habits of Highly Effective People* (pp.235–260). New York: Simon & Schuster.

Chapter 2

1. Elsea, J. G. (1984). *4 Minute Sell.* New York: Simon & Schuster Adult Publishing Group.

2. Elsea, J. G. (1986). *First Impression Best Impression.* New York: Simon & Schuster.

3. "Mirror, mirror—A summary of research findings on body image." http://www.sirc.org/publik/mirror.html

4. American Society for Aesthetic Plastic Surgery. (2005). The American Society for Aesthetic Plastic Surgery 2004 Cosmetic Surgery National Data Bank Statistics. New York: ASAPS Communications Office.

Chapter3

1. Manning, G.L. & Reece, B.L. (1998). *Selling Today Building Quality Partnership.* (8th ed.) Upper Saddle River, NJ: Prentice Hall, Inc.

Chapter 6

1. Elliott, J. (1985). "Frontline: A class divided: An unfinished crusade—an interview with Jane Elliott. http://www.pbs.org/wgbh/pages/frontline/shows/divided/etc/crusade.html

2. Payne, Ruby, K. (2005). *A Framework for Understanding Poverty.* Highlands, TX: aha! Process, Inc.

Chapter 8

1. *The New American Webster Handy College Dictionary,* (3rd ed.). (1995). New York: Penguin Putnam, Inc.

2. Jackson, B. & Hardiman, R. (Rev. by Olsson, J., 1988). "Cycle of Prejudice and Oppression." Tobyhanna, PA: Cultural Bridges.

3. Mosier, J. M. & Wimms-Gadsden, P. (1998). "Valuing Diversity: A Training Curriculum." PA Child Welfare Competency-Based Training and Certification Program. Shippensburg, PA: Shippensburg University.

4. Mosier & Wimms-Gadsden.

5. Mosier & Wimms-Gadsden.

6. Mosier & Wimms-Gadsden.

Chapter 10

1. Payne. (pp. 8-25)

2. Payne. (p. 5)

3. Payne. (p. 7)

4. DiversityInc staff (2006). "Dabbling in Diversity Surveys Is Dangerous" http://www.diversityinc.com/public/19528print.cfm.

5. Assaraf, J. (2003). *The Street Kid's Guide to Having It All.* San Diego, CA: The Street Kid Company.

Chapter 11

1. "Biological Basis of Heredity: Cell Reproduction." http://anthro.palomar.edu/biobasis/bio_2.htm

2. Woodson, C. G. "Carter G. Woodson quotes." http://en.thinkexist.com/quotes/carter_g._woodson/

3. Tzu, S. (1994). *The Art of War* (p. 179). (R. D. Sawyer, Trans.). New York: Barnes and Nobel Books.

4. Ries, A. & Trout, J. (1993). *The 22 Immutable Laws of Marketing* (pp. 10-13). New York: HarperBusiness.

5. Garvey, A. J. (1986). *The Philosophy and Opinions of Marcus Garvey, or, Africa for the Africans* (p. 12). Dover, MA: Majority Press.

6. Tzu, S. p. 179.

7. Gentry, M. (2005, April). *Universal R.E.S.P.E.C.T. Principles.* Paper presented at the Men & Women of R.E.S.P.E.C.T. training, Chicago Heights, IL.

Chapter 12

1. Whybrow, P.C. (2005). *America Mania: When More is Not Enough.* New York: W.W. Norton & Company, Inc.

Chapter 14

1. Hall. *Beyond Culture.*

2. Hall, E.T., Mosier & Wimms-Gadsden.

3. Mosier & Wimms-Gadsden.

Chapter 15

1. Thiederman, S. (2003). *Making Diversity Work* (p. 99). Chicago, IL: Dearborn Trade Publishing.

2. Baldwin, J. & Mead, M. (1971). *A Rap on Race* (pp.25–26). New York: Del Publishing.

3. Gray, J. (1992). *Men Are from Mars, Women Are from Venus.* New York: HarperCollins Publishers.

Chapter 16

1. Altuna, B. "Letter—Diversity Shows Beauty," published 01/12/06 at "The observer & eccentric newspapers, mirror newspapers and hometown weeklies in—www.hometownlife.com—Michigan." http://www.hometownlife.com.

Chapter 18

1. Thiederman, p. 2.

2. DiversityInc staff (2006). "Dabbling in Diversity Surveys Is Dangerous" http://www.diversityinc.com/public/19528print.cfm.

3. Thiederman, p. 2.

4. Blank, R. & Slipp, S. (1994). *Voices of Diversity.* New York: Amacom.

5. Zemke, R., Raines, C. & Filipczak, B. (2000). *Generations at Work: Managing the Clash of Veterans, Boomers, Xers, and Nexters in Your Workplace.* New York: Amacom.

5. Thiederman, p. 81.

6. Glasser, W. (1994) *The Control Theory Manager.* New York: HarperBusiness.

7. Lundin, S. C., Paul, H. & Christensen, J. (2000). *Fish!: A Remarkable Way to Boost Morale and Improve Results.* New York: Hyperion.

Chapter 19
1. Thiederman, pp. 1–3.

2. DiversityInc staff (2006). "Dabbling in Diversity Surveys Is Dangerous" http://www.diversityinc.com/public/19528print.cfm.

3. Thiederman, p. 83.

Chapter 20
1. Mosier & Wimms-Gadsden.

2. Sonnenschein, W. (1999). *The Diversity Toolkit: How You Can Build and Benefit from a Diverse Workforce* (p. 8). Chicago, IL: Contemporary Books.

3. Covey, S. R. (2004). *The 8th Habit* (pp.46–47). New York: Free Press.

4. Gentry, M. (2005, March 31). Men & Women of R.E.S.P.E.C.T. training, Chicago Heights, IL.

5. Burke, E. "Edmond Burke quotes." http://www.brainyquote.com/quotes/quotes/e/edmundburk134243.html.

6. Crane, F. "Frank Crane quotes." http://www.brainyquote.com/quotes/authors/f/frank_crane.html.

Index

H
Hall, Edward, 122
heterosexual privilege, 82
homosexuality, 9, 42, 83, 115, 162
Hurricane Katrina, 36, 56, 80, 140

I
identity development, 49, 89, 91, 94-96
inequity, inequities, 64, 136, 140, 159, 167-168, 181, 192
invisible human characteristics, 12

K
King, Dr. Martin Luther, Jr., 49, 121

M
majority corporate culture-see "corporate culture"
majority privilege, 69, 78-82, 86-87, 94
Malcolm X, 118
media, 2, 11-12, 49, 72, 75, 92, 103, 161
mentors/mentoring, 147-148, 163-164, 168-169, 173, 179, 192
multicultural, 189, 191
myths, 38-40, 43-47, 49, 71-72, 110

O
oppression, 37-38, 43, 59, 67, 69-73, 76-78, 01-92, 182, 187-189

P
peak performance, 104, 179
personal value, 35, 100-102
prejudice, 37-38, 43, 57, 59-67, 69, 71-72, 74-75, 77, 91-92,138, 151, 162, 167, 182, 187-190
primary dimensions of diversity. 9-10
professional development, 171-172

Q
quality relationships, 132, 176, 182

R

race, 2, 9, 36, 39, 69, 72, 75, 81, 89, 92, 94, 119, 132, 140, 150, 157, 175, 182

    race card, 94, 159

    race consciousness, 139

racial identity, 80, 87

racism, 43, 80, 82, 115, 119, 139, 187-188

racist, 23, 36, 50, 74, 82, 134, 162, 187

R.E.S.P.E.C.T., 99, 103

retention, 167, 177

    retention, employee, 177

reverse discrimination, 81, 118

righteousness, 29, 33-34, 37-38,137

S

secondary dimensions of diversity, 9-10

self-evaluate, 177

sexual harassment, 63, 161, 163-164

sexual orientation, 9, 30, 84, 115, 162, 165, 175

similarities, 71, 106, 125, 129, 131-134, 136-138

stereotype/stereotyping, 12, 29-30,36, 43-44, 47, 49-57, 59, 62-63, 71-72, 75-76, 91, 125, 138, 140, 160-162, 183, 190

T

turnover, 144, 176

    turnover, employee, 17, 177

U

unity, 5, 120, 127, 181

V

values, 2-6, 13-17, 21, 27, 29-33, 35-37, 59, 83, 100-101, 116, 154,163, 167, 171, 186

visible characteristics, 11-13, 20